This Wilderness of War

This Wilderness of War

The Civil War Letters of George W. Squier, Hoosier Volunteer

Edited by

Julie A. Doyle,

John David Smith, and

Richard M. McMurry

❧

Voices of the Civil War

Frank L. Byrne,

Series Editor

The University of Tennessee Press / Knoxville

The Voices of the Civil War series makes available a variety of primary source materials that illuminate issues on the battlefield, the home front, and the Western front, as well as other aspects of this historic era. The series contextualizes the personal accounts within the framework of the latest scholarship and expands established knowledge by offering new perspectives, new materials, and new voices.

Frontispiece. George W. Squier, Company D, 44th Indiana Volunteer Infantry. Courtesy of Allen County–Fort Wayne Historical Society.

The paper in this book meets the minimum requirements of the American National Standard for Permanence of Paper for Printed Library Materials.
∞ The binding materials have been chosen for strength and durability.
♲ Printed on recycled paper.

Library of Congress Cataloging-in-Publication Data

Squier, George W. (George Walter), 1831–1907.
This wilderness of war: the Civil War letters of George W. Squier, Hoosier volunteer / edited by Julie A. Doyle, John David Smith, and Richard M. McMurry. — 1st ed.
    p.   cm. — (Voices of the Civil War)
Includes bibliographical references (p.   ) and index.
ISBN 1-57233-006-6 (cloth: alk. paper)
1. Squier, George W. (George Walter), 1831–1907—Correspondence. 2. United States. Army. Indiana Infantry Regiment, 44th (1861–1865) 3. Indiana—History—Civil War, 1861–1865—Personal narratives. 4. Indiana—History—Civil War, 1861–1865—Regimental histories. 5. United States—History—Civil War, 1861–1865—Personal narratives. 6. United States—History—Civil War, 1861–1865—Regimental histories. 7. Soldiers—Indiana—Correspondence. 8. Indiana—Biography. I. Doyle, Julie A. II. Smith, John David, 1949– . III. McMurry, Richard M. IV. Title. V. Series: Voices of the Civil War series.
E506.5 44th.S68 1998
973.7'472'092—dc21
[B]   97-33835

For John and Carolyn Doyle
—J. A. D.

For Thomas H. Appleton Jr. and James C. Klotter
—J. D. S.

For cricket . . . just in case I don't get the other book done.
—R. M. M.

Contents

ↄ

Illustrations

☙

Foreword

໑

George W. Squier was an Indianan born to New England settlers in the northeast-ern part of the Hoosier State. At the start of the Civil War, he had a wife and three young children. Nonetheless, he joined the 44th Indiana in which he rose from cor-poral to first lieutenant. From 1862 to 1865, he wrote regularly and at length to his wife. While her replies do not survive, he obviously expected her not only to wel-come his narrative prose but to appreciate his literary references. Warmly personal, his letters, here well edited, convey affectionate concern for his family and a desire to return home that conflicted with his loyalty to his unit and cause.

As the 44th Indiana participated in major Western battles, Squier described those at Fort Donelson, Shiloh, and Stones River (the latter in graphic detail). About Chick-amauga, he felt he was being repetitious and so was disappointingly concise. In his accounts of battles, Squier was more candid than many soldiers in describing the mutilation of the dead and wounded and in acknowledging the practice of robbing the dead enemy—even admitting that he himself had done it. He also had no criti-cism of the Indianans' enthusiastic foraging for food among the secessionists in Ten-nessee. Still, he took a dim view of the army's vices, especially swearing and gambling. Upon seeing the "snow white tents" lighted up at night, "when I knew how the in-mates of these 'portable dwellings' were spending that beautiful Evening I could but think of those whited Sepulchers which are so fair without but within are dead men's bones."

This fighting Christian reformer (as he doubtless perceived himself) commented often on the moral issues of the war. Regarding secession as evil, he had been willing to enlist to save the Union. When the war turned into one also against slavery after Lincoln's Emancipation Proclamation, he, unlike a number of soldiers from the Old Northwest, came to see it as striking at the root of rebellion. As Republican victory in the state election in Indiana in 1864 foreshadowed Lincoln's reelection, Squier re-joiced "me thinks the Angles of Heaven clap their fair hands in ecstatic delight . . . , [while] Devils tremble for the safety of their kingdom on earth (the southern con-federacy)." Regarding Lincoln as an experienced, selfless leader, Squier opined, "And last but not least, *he is a Christian*." Bitter after Lincoln's assassination, he approv-ingly described the arrest and humiliation of nine men at Chattanooga who had re-joiced at the news—all Democrats, he claimed. Yet he increasingly questioned the course of the more radical Republicans in the summer of 1865. When his wife agreed with their call to enfranchise the blacks whose emancipation he had hailed, Squier opposed such a Federal policy. Thus he exemplified the ambivalent attitudes of white Northern Republicans toward Reconstruction from controversial start to pathetic finish. Ironically, a bold voice of the Civil War became cautious with regard to matters of race.

Frank L. Byrne
Kent State University

Acknowledgments

꩜

The editors acknowledge, with gratitude, the following individuals who assisted them in the preparation of *This Wilderness of War:* Richard Costello, Raleigh, N.C.; Walter Font, Fort Wayne Historical Society; Alexandra Gressitt, Indiana Historical Society; Michelle A. Francis, Department of History and Records Management Services, Presbyterian Church (USA), Montreat, N.C.; Walter B. Hill Jr., National Archives and Records Administration; Stephanie and Bill LaTour, Dearborn, Mich.; Norene Miller, North Carolina State University; Mike Musick, National Archives and Records Administration; Mark E. Neely Jr., St. Louis University; Alan Nolan, Indianapolis; Jim Ogden, Chickamauga–Chattanooga National Battlefield; Gerald J. Prokopowicz, The Lincoln Museum, Fort Wayne, Ind.; Daniel J. Salemson, North Carolina State University; John Selch, Indiana State Library; Dick and Wilda Skidmore, Hanover, Ind.; Sylvia A. Smith, Raleigh, N.C.; Dick B. Sossomon, Raleigh, N.C.; Yvette M. Stillwell, North Carolina State University; Mark Weldon, Fort Wayne, Ind.; Bob Willey, Fort Wayne, Ind.; the reference and interlibrary loan departments, D. H. Hill Library, North Carolina State University; the staff of the U.S. Army Military Institute, Carlisle Barracks, Pa.

Introduction

❧

Indiana sent 208,367 men to suppress what in April 1861 President Abraham Lincoln declared "an insurrection against the Government of the United States." George W. Squier (1831–1907) was one of the thousands of Hoosiers who answered Lincoln's call for volunteers. Squier left a remarkable series of letters to his wife, Ellen, that chronicle the ebb and flow of Civil War army life in the Union Army and provide a highly nuanced view of a Midwestern soldier's day-to-day dreams, longings, and frustrations.[1]

Squier served from 1861 to 1865 in the 44th Indiana Volunteer Infantry. His letters, never before published, provide a treasure trove of military detail for the Western theater and underscore the depth of a Union soldier's love for his family, the Union, and his devotion to antislavery ideology. As the war wore on, however, Squier gradually became disillusioned. Though his letters home always emphasized the pathos of the death and destruction he witnessed, gradually Squier's naïveté turned to cynicism. As Squier moved up through the ranks (he mustered into Company D as a corporal October 20, 1861, was promoted to first lieutenant May 18, 1864, and to captain February 17, 1865), and traveled through the devastated South, he increasingly came to question the war's raison d'être. Thoroughly loyal to the Union and committed to antislavery, Squier nonetheless ultimately became uncomfortable with the results of black liberation and espoused a certain ambivalence toward the cause he had fought so valiantly to uphold. Always honest, direct, pragmatic, and devoted to his family, Squier's letters to Ellen provide a superb window to one soldier's metamorphosis during America's greatest tragedy.[2]

George Walter Squier was the eldest of seven children born to Platt and Aurilla Squier. Platt Squier was born in New York in 1799; Aurilla Goodspeed Squier came from Vermont. After their marriage, Platt and Aurilla moved first to Ohio and then, in 1836, to Allen County, Indiana, in the northeastern part of the state. Along with their two oldest children—George, born September 13, 1831, in Essex County, New York, and Laura, born in 1833—the Squiers settled in Scipio Township, in the extreme northeast corner of Allen County. They were among the pioneer families to settle in Scipio, and their son Lafayette Squier was the first white child born there in 1839.[3]

Scipio Township, located twenty miles northeast of Fort Wayne, was a remote wilderness in the early years of its settlement. According to one historian, the first settlers of this area had to buy supplies in Fort Wayne and float them down the

Maumee River in canoes to the state border, "then pack their provisions on their backs a distance of six miles through a dense wilderness, inhabited only by Indians and innumerable droves of wolves, bears, and wildcats." As more and more settlers arrived, the woods and expanding frontier gradually gave way to farmland and cattle grazing.[4]

Platt Squier was one of the leading pioneers who forged out a farm, and a successful one at that, from the northern Indiana wilderness. Initially clearing more than two hundred acres of land, he came to own as much as fifteen hundred acres. Not surprisingly Platt Squier became a leading member of the local community, serving as justice of the peace in Scipio Township for some twenty-four years. According to one historian of Allen County, Squier ranked as "one of the leading citizens and won the respect of all who knew him. He was friendly to churches and schools and a leader in many laudable enterprises."[5]

According to Indiana census records, by 1860 Platt Squier was a sixty-year-old successful farmer whose real estate was appraised at $8,000. In the same year, his eldest son, George, had acquired a farm of his own, one valued at $1,500. George, who had married Ellen Powers in 1852, had three children by 1860: Wilber, age six; Alice, age four; and Ella, age one. While the federal census taker failed to list Squier's occupation, his later military service record indicates that he was a merchant at the time of his enlistment in the 44th Indiana Volunteer Infantry. He stood five feet, seven and one-half inches tall, was fair complexioned, and had hazel eyes and light hair. The Civil War soon brought the thirty-year-old merchant to a new level of manhood.[6]

In August 1861, Indiana Governor Oliver P. Morton ordered the formation of a camp for volunteers at Fort Wayne, later known as Camp Allen. Hugh B. Reed, who eventually would be commissioned as colonel of the 44th Indiana Volunteer Infantry Regiment, assumed command of the camp. The 30th Indiana Volunteer Regiment was the first unit organized at Camp Allen, but the demand for more troops by the Lincoln administration quickly led to the organization of other regiments. In October 1861, the 30th Indiana Regiment departed Camp Allen for active service and the first volunteers of the 44th Indiana Regiment began to assemble. So few able-bodied men remained in Fort Wayne during the war, that in 1862 the city was forced to disband its recently formed baseball team.[7]

John H. Rerick, M.D. (appointed the 44th Indiana's assistant surgeon September 1861, promoted to surgeon October 1863, and author of the unit's regimental history), reported that residents of Allen County actively participated in recruiting volunteers. By making speeches, participating in public meetings, and circulating enlistment agreements, residents of the Tenth Congressional District encouraged support for their local regiment. By November 1861, volunteers had filled the ranks of the 44th Indiana. Dr. Rerick described the regiment as an exemplary sampling of local Indiana society; most of the volunteers were "young men from the farm and shop, and all, with few exceptions, were in possession of a good common school education, whilst numbers had passed through high school grades, and some had 'been to college.'"[8]

Shortly before the 44th Indiana departed Fort Wayne for active duty, a correspon-

Col. Hugh B. Reed, Commander of the 44th Indiana Volunteer Infantry. Courtesy of Mark Weldon.

dent for the Fort Wayne *Weekly Sentinel* visited Camp Allen. After attending a religious service held for a large group of soldiers, the reporter commented on the general "cleanliness and general good order" of the camp. He found the fresh recruits to be "not only fine-looking men physically, but also respectable, well-behaved and moral, with little or none of that rowdy element too often met with in camps." The enthusiastic reporter concluded that "the 44th will be a model regiment, and a credit to the 10th district and the State of Indiana."[9]

Members of the 44th Indiana Volunteer Infantry. Courtesy of the Massachusetts Commandry, Military Order of the Loyal Legion, and the U.S. Army Military Institute.

The 44th Indiana departed Camp Allen November 23, 1861, amidst great fanfare provided by Fort Wayne's patriotic citizenry. As the local regiment marched through the city's streets to the railroad depot, large crowds cheered them enthusiastically. Stopping in front of the court house, the regiment assembled in formation as Fort Wayne's mayor, F. P. Randall, presented the men with a flag donated by the ladies of the city. Adj. Charles Case, spokesman for the regiment, delivered a brief speech, thanking the men and women of Fort Wayne for their support. According to the *Weekly Sentinel,* Adjutant Case vowed that the flag would never be disgraced. At the conclusion of this ceremony, the regiment boarded a train headed south. Final destination: the loyal slave state, Kentucky.[10]

En route, the 44th Indiana Regiment stopped first in Indianapolis, where it was welcomed by local dignitaries and politicians. The Reverend G. C. Beeks, the first chaplain of the 44th Indiana, wrote a number of letters back to the *Weekly Sentinel,* describing the unit's initial experiences. In the first days after its departure from Fort Wayne, Beeks portrayed the soldiers as a very confident group—a unit that believed in themselves as "the banner regiment of the State." The Reverend Beeks proclaimed that "no officers felt and manifested more interest in a regiment of men than do ours." After Indianapolis, the 44th Indiana moved south en route to Evansville, Indiana, where it was encamped for several weeks. The chaplain reported that the townspeople there greeted his regiment by cheering and firing cannons, as well as by hosting a lavish welcome dinner prepared by the women of Evansville. Duty soon called, however, and the 44th Indiana received orders to march across the Ohio River to Henderson, Kentucky, and to its destiny as one of the Hoosier State's foremost fighting units.[11]

The new soldiers no doubt were apprehensive as they left the friendly confines of Indiana and entered Kentucky, a state known both for its almost universal support of slavery and its split loyalties between the Union and the Confederacy. Untested in battle and far from their homes in northern Indiana, the men of the 44th Indiana were forced to adjust quickly to new circumstances. Dr. Rerick, for example, observed that their first view of slaves shocked many of the men. While the attitudes of white Indianans toward the "peculiar institution" ranged from hatred to indifference, Rerick nevertheless noted that for the Hoosiers "the sight of a slave at daily, unrequited toil was new." From Henderson, the regiment traversed throughout the Commonwealth, first southeast to Calhoun, then northeast to South Carrolton in January 1862, and then back again to Calhoun on February 1. Heavy marching and bad weather took its toll as many of the men became sick. Dr. Rerick reported that pneumonia and typhoid fever were the primary diseases. Lack of proper medical supplies and hospital facilities exacerbated the problem, with the sick relegated to abandoned buildings, taverns, and some private homes. George W. Squier contracted typhoid fever at South Carrolton and was hospitalized at the Division Hospital in Calhoun. This malady contributed to serious medical complications later in Squier's life.[12]

The 44th Indiana first entered combat at Fort Donelson on the Cumberland River in west Tennessee on February 15, 1862. As part of Gen. U. S. Grant's army, Gen. Lew Wallace's 3d Division, the Indiana soldiers found themselves in the thick of the battle. Fifteen percent of the 3d Division's total casualties at Fort Donelson came from the ranks of the 44th Indiana. Several reports filtered back to the *Weekly Sentinel* that described the "coolness and gallantry" of the hometown unit in battle. Having captured two Confederate flags in the fight, the 44th Indiana earned the distinction of flying the first Federal flag over the defeated Confederate fort. The glories of war, however, failed to overcome its grim realities. In a published letter, Chaplain Beeks recounted his experiences aboard a steamer on the Cumberland River. In the absence of the regimental surgeons, Beeks was forced to care for many of the wounded after the battle: "The first and second days I had the wounded of three steamers to see to—extracting balls, amputating fingers, reducing fractures . . . and, in fact, everything you could imagine; and astonishing to tell, all this was done with my old thumb lancet, which I have carried so many years, and my penknife."[13]

The 44th Indiana also played a major role in the next great clash of the Western theater on April 6–7, 1862, at Shiloh on the Tennessee River. As a result of its hard fighting and endurance in this engagement, the regiment earned the sobriquet "the Iron Forty-fourth." Writing to his wife, Colonel Reed expressed his admiration for the behavior of his troops at Pittsburg Landing: "The more I study and learn what the Forty-fourth Regiment really did in this great battle, the more do I admire the gallantry and bravery of the men. At one time they charged the enemy alone, and were the last troops to leave the field on the left wing, on Sunday [April 6]. They marched off in good order, all alone, and far in the rear of the other forces, the enemy following closely behind in over-whelming numbers." The regiment also received accolades in the *Weekly Sentinel* for its courage at Shiloh: "It may be remembered that our gallant 44th regiment . . . withstood for hours the shock of the whole rebel army, and gallantly maintained their ground, while all around them was confusion and dismay." On May 10, 1862, a month after the battle, the *Sentinel* printed an article from a Philadelphia newspaper that argued that the 44th Indiana merited praise for its gallant performance at Shiloh. According to the Pennsylvania paper, "it seems to be universally admitted that the Indiana 44th, Colonel Hugh B. Reed, was *the* regiment of the battle at Pittsburg Landing. They made several of the most brilliant stands in opposition to an overwhelming force. . . . The regiment nobly stood the fiery test, when their companions in arms retired upon either side."[14]

The 44th Indiana's distinguished service at Shiloh, however, came at a high price. The regiment sustained heavy losses: its available forces were reduced from 478 to 280 active men in the battle. Only thirteen Union regiments suffered more casualties at Shiloh than did Squier's unit. As a result, the men felt justified in their opinion that the surprise attack by the Confederates on the morning of April 6 resulted from "gross carelessness and an insufficient system of picketing" by U.S. Army officers.[15]

Following the Battle of Shiloh, the 44th Indiana moved southward and participated in the April–May 1862 siege of Corinth, Mississippi. While encamped near Corinth, the men often were within earshot of Rebel lines. In a letter home, dated May 26, 1862, Cpl. Alfred Shields of Company G described his experiences in camp:

> We are now within 3 miles of Corinth and can hear the rebel drums in their camps. Our pickets and the Rebs are within a few hundred yards of each other and some times they "Holler" at each other. Yesterday our regiment was on picket duty and Lt. Grim of our regt. went and talked with a Rebel capt. . . . We have been building works during the past wk. in front of our camp and cutting out the underbrush. Much hard work the whole time. I am on duty every other day with some drill every day. We expect a hard fight, but can thrash the Rebs in fine style.[16]

In June 1862, the regiment left Corinth, moving northward to Battle Creek, Tennessee. According to Dr. Rerick, the march "was much complained of by the soldiers on account of the lack of full rations, and of insufficient clothing. The last part of the journey was performed by many barefooted." The regiment's next engagement came on October 8, 1862, at the Battle of Perryville, Kentucky, where it played an insignificant role.[17] After numerous marches and countermarches through Kentucky and Tennessee, the regiment went into winter quarters at Nashville, Tennessee, on November 30, 1862. According to Dr. Rerick, the 44th Indiana had traveled almost seven hundred miles since leaving Battle Creek on August 20. During this time the soldiers "were without shelter of any kind, carried but one blanket apiece, and were nearly all the time on half rations, and very poorly shod." Corporal Shields of Company G agreed. Writing home, he complained, "We do not have such a thing as tents. In fact we have not been inside of a tent since leaving Battle Creek, but I do hope that we will draw our tents before winter sets in rough."[18]

Once encamped at Nashville, the men of the 44th Indiana learned of Colonel Reed's resignation. Before his departure, they presented him with the regimental flag given them by the citizens of Fort Wayne. Colonel Reed responded by providing the regiment with a new flag. Capt. William C. Williams of Company G took Reed's place.[19]

The regiment next saw action at Stones River from December 31, 1862, to January 2, 1863. On the first day, the 44th Indiana, as part of Col. Edward Pierce Fyffe's brigade, was caught in a crossfire while marching across an open field. In a letter published in the *Sentinel* after the battle, a member of the regiment expressed amazement that his unit avoided suffering overwhelming casualties: "All old soldiers, especially of the first line, agree in saying that they would prefer hours of the hardest Shiloh fighting, to the fifteen or twenty minutes occupied in falling back across that open field [at Stones River], yet the regiment seemed to be under the kind care of a protecting Providence, for the loss in proportion to the exposure was not large."

After a quiet January 1, 1863, the 44th Indiana took part in repulsing an enemy attack on the second day of the new year. In that fight, fifty-eight Union cannon played a key role in defeating a Confederate charge. According to Dr. Rerick, "A battle scene ensued that hardly had a parallel during the war." The musketry and artillery fire was so intense, Rerick recalled, that "[t]he earth trembled under the shock," and "window-glass was broken by the concussion of the air two miles distant." The Union troops repulsed the Rebels and "the Forty-fourth planted its colors on the enemy's breastworks, and slept that night on the field of battle." The regiment lost about sixty of its three hundred men in the battle. Unfortunately, the regiment's newly minted colonel, William C. Williams, was captured during the battle and, after spending several months at Libby Prison in Richmond, Virginia, he was exchanged. Williams returned to the regiment briefly but resigned on July 27, 1863. Col. Simeon C. Aldrich replaced him. In November 1863, Colonel Aldrich was appointed provost marshal of Chattanooga, Tennessee.[20]

As part of the Army of the Cumberland, the 44th Indiana entered winter quarters at Murfreesboro, Tennessee, on January 5, 1863. It remained there without significant military action for the next six months. According to Dr. Rerick, this period was a quiet but also troubling time for the regiment. While the men had relatively comfortable quarters, good medical facilities, and only light duties to perform, the regiment's morale nonetheless began to wane. Disaffection set in among some of the men. The length of the war, its uncertain outcome, and the increasing civilian opposition to the war back home all exacerbated discontent in the ranks. News from Indiana about secret antiwar organizations—such as the Knights of the Golden Circle, headquartered there—undermined the regiment's morale. Dr. Rerick nonetheless believed that the majority of the men of the 44th Indiana supported the Lincoln government's prosecution of the war and opposed the efforts of the Indiana state legislature to deprive Governor Morton of his constitutional right to act as commander in chief of the state militia. He cited, for example, the regiment's unanimous approval of a resolution presented to the Indiana senate on February 12, 1863, that affirmed its complete and unconditional support for the war.[21]

This apparently enthusiastic endorsement of the war contrasted with the opinions expressed in several published letters early in 1863. Written by unidentified soldiers of the 44th Indiana from their camp at Murfreesboro, the letters appeared in the *Sentinel,* a Democratic paper, shortly after the war had been redefined by the Emancipation Proclamation. These men had signed up to keep the Union intact, not to liberate the South's slaves.

One member of Company B, for example, complained, "The soldier beholds himself fighting for a thing that he did not contract for, to wit, to free negroes. This last feature has caused our armies to relinquish their zeal in the further prosecution of the war." Another soldier stated bluntly that the men "have become disgusted with the [Lincoln] administration, and are completely discouraged in the further prosecution of this war. . . . We did not hire ourselves to this government to *free negroes,* and we do not wish to see thousands of our own race fall by disease and in battle to sustain that famous proclamation." This disgruntled Hoosier also complained that the regiment suffered from inadequate clothing, housing, and rations and that it had not been paid in six months. He concluded that "the universal sentiment is, that an armistice be agreed to without delay, to restore peace, as we are all well satisfied that peace cannot be restored in any other way." In a similar vein, another letter championed the Democratic party as the best hope for ending the war and the sufferings of the soldiers, who were "undergoing privations such as no civilized people on the globe should do, and all to free the nigger."[22]

In late June 1863, the 44th Indiana moved from Murfreesboro to McMinnville, Tennessee, as part of a movement against the command of Confederate Gen. Braxton Bragg. During the next few months the regiment performed escort and guard duties, participated in several raids, and built fortifications. In September, the Indiana soldiers broke camp and traveled over 130 miles to take part in the Battle of Chickamauga. Now under the command of Lt. Col. Simeon C. Aldrich, the 44th Indiana faced hard fighting at Chickamauga September 18–20 and again on September 22 at Missionary Ridge. In their official reports, generals Thomas L. Crittenden, Horatio P. Van Cleve, and Thomas J. Wood commended the 44th Indiana Regiment for its performance at Chickamauga. However, the seventy-four casualties suffered by the regiment were relatively light when compared to its losses at Shiloh and Stones River.[23]

After the battles, the 44th Indiana encamped near Missionary Ridge. When the Confederates succeeded in cutting off Union supply lines for a time, the regiment endured a short-lived siege. The men received half-rations at first, then one-third, then one-fourth, and eventually none at all. According to Dr. Rerick, however, the regiment always managed to maintain its reputation for keeping its haversacks full. He referred to a story that the soldiers of the 44th Indiana "could pick up a sheep grazing in the fields by the wayside, skin, dress, and divide it up among them without missing step in the march." When the siege ended in late November 1863, the regiment received a new assignment. A reorganization of the Army of the Cumberland had placed Maj. Gen. George H. Thomas in command, and, in the ensuing changes, Lieutenant Colonel Aldrich of the 44th Indiana was appointed provost marshal of Chattanooga. Here the regiment began post duty in November.[24]

In December 1863, 220 members of the 44th Indiana reenlisted. As a result, the regiment was termed a veteran volunteer regiment and each reenlisted man received a $400 bounty and a thirty-day furlough. The citizens of Fort Wayne eagerly awaited the unit's return home. Announcing the soldiers' expected arrival, the *Sentinel* declared that the regiment had "seen much hard service" but had "gained imperishable laurels, reflecting honor on the state and especially on the 10th District." The furloughed troops reached Fort Wayne on January 31, 1864. At a public reception held in their honor, the soldiers enjoyed a meal prepared by the ladies of Fort Wayne and heard speeches of praise and thanks from leading citizens. The 44th Indiana then marched through the city bearing the battle-scarred flags that it had carried throughout the war. The *Sentinel* reported that the men appeared fit and "were without exception the neatest, best looking, and best behaved body of troops we have seen since this war commenced."[25]

The regiment rendezvoused at Kendallville, Indiana, on March 10, 1864. With some 150 new recruits, the veterans returned to their post in Chattanooga. As the base of operation for supplies moving south, as well as a point of concentration for troops, Chattanooga was a linchpin in the Union army's war machine. The 44th Indiana enjoyed good conditions while in camp there. In several letters to his wife, Dr. Edward B. Speed, an assistant surgeon with the regiment, described camp life in July 1864: "Chattanooga is more of a place than I expected to fin[d] it. It is a most busy place I ever saw. There is every thing going on here you can think of. Our camp is on a hill in the north east part of the town, high and pleasant. There is a cool breeze here all of the time." According to Speed, meals at the Chattanooga camp were particularly hearty: "we have plenty of potatoes, bread, crackers, butter beans, pork (as good as any I ever saw), some fresh beef, onions, cucumbers, some ripe apples (but they are rather scarce), codfish, coffee, tea, sugar, condensed milk. . . ." The 44th Indiana remained on duty in Chattanooga for the rest of the war until it was mustered out of service in September 1865. George W. Squier was among the 670 enlisted men and 35 officers who left the service. Only 193 enlisted men and 3 officers from the original members of the regiment were present at war's end, however.[26] The war took its toll on Squier, like on so many soldiers. He left military service with vivid memories of death, destruction, and heroism. Writing in September 1864, Squier admitted to Ellen his desire "to leave this wilderness of war and . . . enjoy the society of the loved ones at home." His discharge came one year later, suffering from chronic "lung trouble and liver disease." This resulted from Squier's 1862 bout with typhoid fever, which plagued him for the remainder of his life. Squier received a small invalid pension from the U.S. government beginning in September 1865.[27]

೮ා

George W. Squier left surprisingly few clues to his life after the war. But no doubt his experiences in the 44th Indiana, like those of hundreds of thousands of veterans of other units, north and south, were defining moments in his life.

According to Squier's military pension records, he returned to Allen County briefly upon his military discharge. About seven months later, he and his family moved to Pleasant Hill, Cass County, in western Missouri, where they lived for the next seven years. The 1870 Cass County census recorded that Squier was a farmer with real estate valued at $3,500. Though generally prosperous, Squier remained hampered by physical pain, the lingering effects of his hospitalization with typhoid fever in Kentucky. In 1882, an examining surgeon reported that Squier was 50 percent incapacitated from performing manual labor because of his lung ailment and predicted that the veteran's disability would worsen over time. Throughout the 1880s, Squier applied unsuccessfully for increases to his invalid pension.[28]

In 1883, the Squiers returned to Allen County, Indiana, residing there for four years before moving to South Haven, Van Buren County, Michigan, in 1887. Located in Michigan's southwest corner, South Haven Township was an agricultural community known especially for its fruit-raising. Here, Ellen Squier died on December 23, 1890, of rectal cancer. Her husband remained a widower until his marriage to the forty-four-year-old Helen Maynard on January 13, 1892. The couple resided in South Haven for the next thirty years.[29]

Squier farmed during these decades, owning seventy acres of land in 1895. He continued to suffer physically from chronic lung disease. By 1897, Squier could not engage in active work for more than two hours per day because of his heart trouble and what an examining surgeon described as "general weakness." On April 2, 1907, Squier was diagnosed with pneumonia. He died eight days later from complications associated with heart disease and was buried at Long View Cemetery, South Haven.[30]

❧

Though George W. Squier may remain obscure in the overall picture of the Civil War, his observations and interpretations of the meaning of the war provide an important primary source and lend support to the recent work of historians Reid Mitchell and James M. McPherson on the Weltanschauung of the common soldier.[31] The war not only separated hundreds of thousands of men from their families and careers, but also forced them to reassess their reasons for participating in the conflict. Like most Civil War soldiers who wrote to their loved ones at home, Squier commented often on the mundane and the meaningful, the various forces that shaped his transformation from a civilian to a volunteer soldier.

Typical of combat soldiers everywhere, Squier devoted much of the contents of his letters to describing the world of war.[32] It was, Squier reminded Ellen a month following Gen. Robert E. Lee's surrender at Appomattox, "[f]our years of blood and death, of sufferings and hardships untold." Squier dodged bullets, watched men die, faulted his officers, and complained frequently of "the dull monotony of camp life" and his plain rations. He wrote often about his loneliness and his eagerness for mail

from home. Squier commented frequently about the weather, the inevitable inanimate enemy of the soldier—rain, storms, mud, cold, and heat. He also expressed deep
concern about his family members, asking questions about their health, economic
security, and sending instructions to his wife and three children. Squier's letters also
document such routine aspects of army life as gambling, swearing, and pilfering the
bodies of the dead. Though the former three offended his Victorian sensibilities, in
the end Squier also rifled the pockets of dead enemy soldiers as did those comrades
he chided for the same offense. On a happier note, his letters brim with pride of his
state and the 44th Indiana regiment. Though his letters contain spelling and gram-
matical errors, Squier nevertheless wrote with clarity and precision. He had a keen,
perceptive mind and strong opinions.

He believed, for example, that the Confederacy had committed treason. Squier
joined the 44th Indiana to suppress the South's rebellion and to uphold the Union.
"Secession," he wrote, "is death—distruction—ruin—evrything good and pure and
holy is blasted and blackened by contact with it." In another letter, Squier remarked
that "Sodom and Gommora seceded from the govern[ment] of high Heaven and
they likewise were punished for their secession." Squier also subscribed clearly to what
historians Eric Foner and David Brion Davis, respectively, have termed the "free labor ideology" and the "slave power conspiracy."[33] "For however we may try to avoid
the fact," Squier wrote Ellen in October 1864, "slavery (mind when I speak of slavery I mean the system of oppression practiced by the southern *gentleman*—not the
negro, for the nergo is no moore responsible for this war than is the steel blade which
the assassin plunges into the heart of his victim responsible for the deed of murder)
is the cause of all of our troubles." Slavery and its white defenders, then, according
to Squier, had to be extinguished. "I would have this a *free* country," he added. "It
needs no argument other than common sense to point the inconsistency of a free
government resting even partially upon the basis of slave labor." Squier considered
slavery's demise so essential to the future of the republic that he wrote: "Slavery must
disappear from our constitution and statute books, or this country dies." "For more
than thirty years," he added, "we have submitted—tamely submitted to a despotism
less tolerant than the absolutism of ancient France or the moore ancient autocracy
. . . of Russia."

Though devoted to the Union cause, the war nonetheless took its toll on Squier.
Shortly after the Shiloh campaign, he admitted doubting his "fervor" and "courage"
to fight. Squier added, however, "I am not sorry I enlisted in the service of my country and most assuredly I am not sorry I enlisted in the service of my God. I find *Great*
comfort and consolation therein." Still, Squier, like many Northerners, was frustrated
by the Union Army's seeming ineptitude, its inability to crush the Confederates, its
poor leadership, and the corruption within Lincoln's administration.

In November 1862, Squier confided to Ellen his shattered idealism. He was out-
raged by "the deception, the low dispisable cunning used to gain position and profit,
I have to clentch my hands," he admitted, "to prevent my patriotism coming out at
the ends of my fingers. I can hardly feel like cursing this government, but the way

the affairs of this nation is conducted—merit is not respected; a man's rights is not recognisced; men are dogs. Shoulder straps and money are *Deities*—they rule this nation." Three months later, in February 1863, Squier expressed his reservations about continuing to fight for the Union cause. He admitted to Ellen:

> I am *sick* of soldiering, and consequently time drags heavily along. Not that our government is worth less than Twelve months ago, but when I know that this war [is] carried on for money making and other selfish purposes, [and] when the majority cares not two straws for the government, I certainly do not feel like exposing my life, ruining my health, and enduring all the hardships of military life. You need not fear that I shal so far forget my duty to my family as to desert, but in case of another fight—if ther is a chance of "playing out"—I do not know what I may do. One thing is very sure— the day is past when there is any honor to be gained in fighting.

In the same month, Squier obviously was depressed and distressed over the failure of the Union armies and with disloyalty among Copperheads and "peace" Democrats back home. "Ruin, complete and utter ruin, stares us in the face," he lamented.

> Our once proud and happy Nation is today toppling over into the abyss of Eternal distruction. The day is forever past when it was an honor to be called an American citizen. We are fast becoming a byword among the nations of the Earth. You think me excited! That I have little or no real grounds for my fears! Perhaps so—but what means that great and rapidly increasing so-called peace party of the North! What means the daily increasing discontent among the soldiers! And what means an armed mob in the state of Indiana for the avowed purpose of resisting the law!

In October 1863, Squier asked Ellen's advice about the merits of his reenlisting in his beloved 44th. He questioned whether it was his duty to do so "while there are so many at home who have not done their part." Squier interpreted Union defeats and military stagnation as evidence of God's displeasure with what he termed "our great national sins."

Though Squier often expressed his impatience with Lincoln, the Hoosier volunteer still supported the president's Emancipation Proclamation and, in general, his transforming of the war from one to suppress a rebellion to one that liberated the South's slaves. Writing in September 1864, Squier informed Ellen that "the government surely has a claim on every able bodied loyal man until the great end is attained, the mighty work accomplished, and the redemption of the enthralled complete, and we become not only in name but in *reality* a free people, and we can consistently claim that America ofers an asylum for the opressed of *all nations*, not excluding even Africa, until even the despised negro can find safety and liberty under [the] broad folds of the American baner." Squier favored Lincoln in the 1864 presidential election because of his experience, his commitment to the Union, his devotion to Christianity, and his antislavery policies.

Squier's enthusiasm for the broad effects of emancipation waned, however, by war's end. In the last letter printed in this edition, written to Ellen from Chattanooga, Tennessee, in July 1865, he disagreed with her regarding the merits of black suffrage. Open to disagreeing with his wife on this and other questions, Squier remarked: "We need never expect to be of one mind in all respects, however desireable it may seem. Individuals of different education and different temperament must sometimes necessarily look at things in [a] different light and consequently arrive at different conclusions." The issue that spirited this intellectual debate between George and Ellen was what Squier considered the manipulation of the question of black voting rights by politicians on both sides of the Mason-Dixon line during presidential Reconstruction.

In George's opinion, politicians and abolitionists wanted to transform Union victory and black liberation into black elevation. They considered "[t]he [mere] supremacy of the law haveing been established" insufficient. He disagreed. Squier doubted that blacks were "our equals in *politics* nor can they become so except by Legislation in the states in which they reside."[34] The exchange between George and Ellen occurred at a time when leading Indiana politicians, most notably Governor Morton, publicly opposed black suffrage. Speaking in Richmond, Indiana, on September 29, 1865, Governor Morton asked: "Can you conceive that a body of men, white or black, who, as well as their ancestors, have been in this condition [as slaves], are qualified to be lifted immediately from their present state into the full exercise of political power . . . ?"[35]

Squier agreed with Morton's position and objected to the radical Republicans' determination *"to organize a hybrid party on the platform of Negro suffrage."* So eager were they to enfranchise the freedmen, Squier argued, radicals—even Chief Justice of the Supreme Court Salmon P. Chase—offered former Confederates a lenient Reconstruction policy in return for providing voting rights for the ex-slaves in the South's revised state constitutions. Though he opposed slavery and welcomed emancipation, Squier nevertheless resented the preferential treatment afforded the freed slaves by the government while white Southerners were discriminated against. Squier objected to "the undue importance or rather *promine[n]ce* that is being given at the present time to every little incident that can be turned into a charge of hatred of an oppressor toward the freedmen." Like his father, Platt Squier, George believed that the Republicans suffered from what he termed "Nigger on the braine." Having fought long and hard for the Union and for emancipation, George Squier considered the notion of black political equality one of the more bitter of "the fruits of war."

℘

Throughout the editing of *This Wilderness of War,* the editors have sought to retain the original intent, meaning, and integrity of George W. Squier's Civil War letters as closely as possible. The letters are deposited at the Lincoln Museum, Fort Wayne,

Indiana, and the editors thank the Lincoln National Life Insurance Company for its kind permission to publish them in this form.

In terms of emendations, the editors have adopted a conservative, "near-literal" editorial style. They have interrupted Squier's prose as infrequently as possible, ever sensitive to infringing upon Squier's authorship, his moods, his time, his place. Nonetheless, for the convenience of the modern reader, the editors have added punctuation and paragraphing when necessary; added capitalization at beginning of sentences; added words or letters in square brackets [ ] when the meaning of the phrase or sentence was not clear; added a question mark in square brackets [?] if a word was illegible; added four bracketed dots [. . . .] for an incomplete sentence; added correct spellings of personal names in square brackets [ ] when Squier misspelled them; and employed angled brackets < > to indicate when a page was torn. The editors refrained from correcting Squier's misspellings or random capitalizations. Throughout, our intent has been to represent as faithfully as possible Squier's words and emotions, not ours.

NOTES

1. W. H. H. Terrell, *Indiana in the War of the Rebellion: Report of the Adjutant General* (Indianapolis, 1960; reprint of vol. 1 of eight-volume report, 1869), 563; Roy P. Basler, ed., *The Collected Works of Abraham Lincoln,* vol. 4 (New Brunswick, N.J., 1953), 338.

2. John H. Rerick, *The Forty-fourth Indiana Volunteer Infantry, History of Its Service in the War of the Rebellion and a Personal Record of Its Members* (Lagrange, Ind., 1880), 165.

3. B. J. Griswold, *The Pictorial History of Fort Wayne, Indiana* (Chicago, 1917), 674.

4. John C. W. Bailey, *Allen County Gazetteer, Containing a Directory of Fort Wayne City, and Historical and Descriptive Sketches of the Several Townships of the County* (Chicago, 1867), 23.

5. *Valley of the Upper Maumee River, with Historical Account of Allen County and the City of Fort Wayne, Indiana. The Story of Its Progress from Savagery to Civilization,* vol. 1 (Madison, Wis., 1889), 382.

6. Population Schedule, Eighth Census of the United States, 1860, Allen County, Indiana, 460–61; Indiana Works Progress Administration, *Index to Marriage Records, Allen County, Indiana, 1824–1920* (1938), 1602; George W. Squier Compiled Military Service Record, Record Group 109, National Archives and Records Administration, Washington, D.C.; George W. Squier Pension Records, Record Group 15, National Archives and Records Administration, Washington, D.C.

7. Rerick, *The Forty-fourth Indiana Volunteer Infantry,* 7–8; Emma Lou Thornbrough, *Indiana in the Civil War Era, 1850–1880* (Indianapolis, 1965), 702. The companies of the 44th Indiana Volunteer Regiment came from Indiana's Tenth Congressional District. This consisted of eight counties in the northeastern part of the state: Elkhart, Kosciusko, Whitley, Noble, Lagrange, Steuben, De Kalb, and Allen. See Yvette M. Stillwell, "The Forty-fourth Indiana Volunteer Regiment" (unpublished paper, North Carolina State University, 1995), 1.

8. Rerick, *The Forty-fourth Indiana Volunteer Infantry,* 8, 11.

9. *Fort Wayne Weekly Sentinel,* Oct. 26, 1861.

10. Rerick, *The Forty-fourth Indiana Volunteer Infantry*, 15; *Fort Wayne Weekly Sentinel*, Nov. 30, 1861.

11. *Fort Wayne Weekly Sentinel*, Nov. 30, Dec. 7, 1861; Rerick, *The Forty-fourth Indiana Volunteer Infantry*, 20.

12. Rerick, *The Forty-fourth Indiana Volunteer Infantry*, 25, 30–31; George W. Squier Pension Records, RG 15. On the racial attitudes of white Indianans and the heightening of wartime racial friction, see Emma Lou Thornbrough, *The Negro in Indiana Before 1900: A Study of a Minority* (Indianapolis, 1957; reprint, Bloomington, Ind., 1993), 183–205. On epidemics and medical evacuations in this military theater, see Peter Josyph, ed., *The Wounded River: The Civil War Letters of John Vance Lauderdale, M.D.* (East Lansing, Mich., 1993), 20–24.

13. Stillwell, "The Forty-fourth Indiana Volunteer Regiment," 6; *Fort Wayne Weekly Sentinel*, Mar. 1, 1862.

14. Rerick, *The Forty-fourth Indiana Volunteer Infantry*, 52, 55; *Fort Wayne Weekly Sentinel*, Apr. 19, May 10, 1862.

15. Stillwell, "The Forty-fourth Indiana Volunteer Regiment," 13; Rerick, *The Forty-fourth Volunteer Indiana Infantry*, 60.

16. Stillwell, "The Forty-fourth Indiana Volunteer Regiment," 13; Alfred Shields, letter to brother, May 26, 1862, Alfred Shields Papers, Indiana Historical Society. Lieutenant Grim is unidentifiable in all regimental records.

17. James Lee McDonough, *War in Kentucky: From Shiloh to Perryville* (Knoxville, 1994), 378–79, cites the participation of twenty-five Indiana infantry regiments, but not the 44th.

18. Rerick, *The Forty-fourth Indiana Volunteer Infantry*, 64, 74; Shields to his mother, Oct. 31, 1862, Shields Papers.

19. Rerick, *The Forty-fourth Indiana Volunteer Infantry*, 75–76.

20. Stillwell, "The Forty-fourth Indiana Volunteer Regiment," 15; *Fort Wayne Weekly Sentinel*, Jan. 31, 1863.

21. Rerick, *The Forty-fourth Indiana Volunteer Infantry*, 85–88.

22. *Fort Wayne Weekly Sentinel*, Feb. 28, Mar. 14, 1863.

23. Rerick, *The Forty-fourth Indiana Volunteer Infantry*, 96; Stillwell, "The Forty-fourth Indiana Volunteer Regiment," 22–23.

24. Rerick, *The Forty-fourth Indiana Volunteer Infantry*, 101–2, 104–5, 131.

25. Rerick, *The Forty-fourth Indiana Volunteer Infantry*, 106; *Fort Wayne Weekly Sentinel*, Jan. 30, Feb. 6, 1864.

26. A total of 2,203 men served in the 44th Indiana. For a complete distribution of its personnel, see Terrell, *Indiana in the War of the Rebellion*, 561.

27. Rerick, *The Forty-fourth Indiana Volunteer Infantry*, 108–9; Edward B. Speed to Esther Speed, July 12, 26, 1864, Edward B. Speed Papers, Indiana Historical Society; Rerick, *The Forty-fourth Indiana Volunteer Infantry*, 123; George W. Squier Pension Records, RG 15.

28. George W. Squier Compiled Military Service Record, RG 109; Population Schedule, Ninth Census of the United States, 1870, Cass County, Missouri, 25.

29. George W. Squier Pension Records, RG 15; *History of Berrien and Van Buren Counties, Michigan* (Philadelphia, 1880), 533.

30. Van Buren County Plat Book, South Haven Township, 1895; George W. Squier Pension Records, RG 15; "Mr. Squier Buried Friday Afternoon," *South Haven (Mich.) Tribune-Messenger,* Apr. 19, 1907. Helen Squier received George's military pension from 1907 until her death on October 13, 1933.

31. See Mitchell, *Civil War Soldiers: Their Expectations and Their Experiences* (New York, 1988) and *The Vacant Chair: The Northern Soldier Leaves Home* (New York, 1993), and McPherson, *What They Fought For, 1861–1865* (Baton Rouge, 1994).

32. The editorial statement that appears at the conclusion of the introduction explains the editors' rendition of Squier's texts.

33. See Foner, *Free Soil, Free Labor, Free Men: The Ideology of the Republican Party before the Civil War* (New York, 1970); Davis, *The Slave Power Conspiracy and the Paranoid Style* (Baton Rouge, 1969).

34. Though the subject of the beginning of this passage of Squier's letter is incomplete, it is obvious from context that he referred to the freedmen.

35. As a U.S. senator, Morton later reversed his position on black suffrage. Indiana's ratification of the Fifteenth Amendment in 1869 in effect nullified the state's restriction of the suffrage to whites. The state's blacks actively supported Republican candidates as early as 1870. See Thornbrough's *Indiana in the Civil War Era,* 229, and *The Negro in Indiana Before 1900,* 248–54.

*The Civil War Letters
of George W. Squier,
Hoosier Volunteer*

Chapter 1. 1862

✑

LETTER 1

Camp Near Calhoun, Ky. Jan. 12, '62

My own Dear Ellen,

It is Sabbath morning and I write partly for my own comfort and partly thinking you may possibly get it as it seems by your 4th letter rcd. [received] 11th inst that the transmission of letters from camp to Halls Corners is among the things that were. But I'l continue writing at all events though it does seem hard you should not hear from [me] oftener. This is I think the 6th or 7th letter I [have] written to you since we left Camp Allen[1] and you have rcd. but 3 so I have but little courage to write. We struck our tents and took up our line of march for Calhoune on Thursday, Jan. 2 [at] 12 o'clok noon. [We] march[ed] 6 ½ miles, rained [?]. [In the] P.M. [we] pitched tents [and] had plenty straw for beds. And so our march continued day after day through rain and mud, up and down hills, and [we] finally reached this place on Monday last. But I suppose Brother Platt[2] gave you a dicerption [description] of the country over which we passed, allso our camping ground, so I will not. I stood my march very well until Sundy afternoon when I "kinder give out." I was all day Monday travelling 6 mils without Knapsack, canteen or gun but I finally got into camp. [I] grunted round severall days but am now nearly as good as new. But in our trials it is a comfort to know that there is a strong hand to uphold us, a kind Father to care for us, an Allmighty power to protect us in time of peril. I feel that I would not give my hope of Heaven for all the world and all it holds. I know very well I do many things which I ought not to—"But I see another law in my members warring against the law of my mind and bringing me into captivity to the law of sin which is in my members."[3]

It is now nine o'clock and Orderly Moffet[4] passes dow[n] the broad street and cries out "inspection of armes at 10 o'clock." So we have to clean our muskets, brush our pants and jackets and caps, [and] be ready at the roll of the drums to appear in line in apple pie order, so no more at present.

The weather has been cloudy but not cold. Roads rather bad. Citizens strong union and of cours very friendly to the boys. The health of the regiment is very good. The 44 is said to be the "star" regiment of this brigade.[5] Now Dear one should you get this let me assure you that you are *not forgotten*. I think of you many, very many times every day and allways remember you and the dear little ones far away before our Father who careth for all his children. Now Wilber and Allice you must keep in good spirits. Bee good children (I know you will be) and learn to read and spell. Be kind to Ellie. In fact be good children generally. Kiss mama and Ellie for papa and right here —————— I send a kiss to you both.

I hardly know what [I've] written and do[n't] know that it makes much difference if you are to get one letter that I write but I'l write any how as long as I have the means to pay postage.

Good by my Dear ones and remember me as ever your affectionate

George

1. Camp Allen, where the regiment organized, was in Fort Wayne, in what is now Swinney Park. For a brief description of the wartime installation, see M. B. Butler, *My Story of the Civil War and the Under-ground Railroad* (Huntington, Ind., 1914), 27–28.
2. Pvt. Platt J. Squier ("Squyers" in the official roster of Company D), George's brother, who was mortally wounded April 6, 1862, at Shiloh. See Letters 5, 6, 7, and 8.

   Unless otherwise stated, all information in the notes relating to the service of individual soldiers is taken from *Report of the Adjutant General of the State of Indiana* (Indianapolis, 1865–66) [The 44th Indiana is covered in vol. 2 (officers of the regiment) and vol. 5 (enlisted men of the regiment)] or the *Army Register of the Volunteer Forces* (reprint, Gaithersburg, Md., 1987) [vol. 7 covers Indiana units].
3. Rom. 7:23.
4. Either Pvt. Thomas R. Moffet, Company A; Pvt. David D. Moffett, Company H; or 1st Sgt. Thomas C. Moffett, Company D.
5. The regiment was then in what was designated the 13th Brigade, 5th Division, Army of the Ohio. The other regiments in the brigade were the 31st Indiana and the 17th and 25th Kentucky. In February 1862, the brigade became the 1st Brigade, 3d Division, Army of the Tennessee. In March 1862, it was reassigned as the 3d Brigade, 4th Division, Army of the Tennessee.

LETTER 2

Carrollton Ky. Jan. 16, 1862

My own Dear Ellen,

We left Calhoune 4 P.M. yesterday and arrived at this place 6 P.M. same day, a distance of about twenty-five mils up green river. Carrollton is situated on an eminece on the left bank [of] Green river. Has been a beautiful village of some five Hundre[d] inhabitants but is now desolate and deserted. There is not moore than two hud. [hundred] inhabitants now. Such is the fruits of war. We Co D are now quartered in a large Church. [We have] two good stoves [and] plenty of coal so you percive we are right at home. We shal not probaly stay her[e] moore than a few days until the ballanc[e] of our Brigade comes up. Three regiments, the 25 Ky., 31st & 44 Ind., came up last night. Three reg. of infantry & twelve hund. cavalry are expected here to night. We shal probably have some fighting to do before long as we shal now make our way I presume to Nashville, Tenn. and on our way clean out Hopkinsvill, Bowle Green [Bowling Green], &c&c. But then I presume you will not receive this scrawl as I have written so many that has not went through, so it makes little difference whether I write litt[le] or much. But it is some comfort to write because I think it *may* reach you. My health is quite good. The health of the regiment is decidedly better as the measles have had its run. We may now expect less names on the "sick list."[1] I will continue to write. Give my love to all the friends (especially *Mother* & Father). Have Charly write.[2] A kiss ———— for Wilber, Allice and *Ellie* (dear creatures, wouldn't I like to see them) and one especially for ———— yourself. *I have not forgotten you.*

George

I am not sorry I enlisted in the service of my country and most assuredly I am not sorry I enlisted in the service of my God. I find *Great* comfort and consolation therein. May Heaven's blessings rest on the Dear "folks at Home." Once moore good by.

G.W. Squier

Direct as usual

1. Newly organized units usually experienced outbreaks of such diseases as measles because men from isolated rural areas had not been exposed to such ailments prior to going into the army. The death rate from these diseases was high. Rerick noted that soon after the 44th Indiana left Fort Wayne, the sick list "now began to increase rapidly." In mid-January, he wrote, "the sick list was fearfully increased," with 186 men "taken sick during the month." *The Forty-fourth Indiana Volunteer Infantry,* 20, 30, 32–33. See also Butler, *Story,* 57–58, 70.

    Squier himself fell victim to typhoid fever and spent much of January and February 1862 and part of March in the hospital in Calhoun. For this reason he missed the regiment's first fight at Fort Donelson. Squier never completely recovered from this bout with illness and was troubled by a cough resulting from it for years after the war. In 1882, a surgeon who examined him in connection with his application for a military pension found that the 1862 illness had rendered him "one half (½) incapacitated for obtaining his subsistence from manual labor." The doctor concluded that the disability "will probably increase."

2. "Charly" is unidentified. The context makes it clear that he was a relative or friend in Indiana. Perhaps he was the person referred to as "Charlie" in Letter 4.

LETTER 3

Carrollton, Ky. Jan. 17, '61 [1862]

Dear Ellen,

I wrote you a few lines yesterdy but as I wanted to write to C. thought I'd put in a word for you. I'm going to try the experiment of not prepaying the postage and see whether my letters will not go through better.[1]

There will be by tonight a force of fifteen thousand men—Twelve Hundred cavalry besides an efficient battery of artillery—at this place, so you perceive we are able to stand "secesh" a pretty good brush. Thare was a "secesh" flag captured this morning. Several "secesh" are now held in custody.

A few of the war prices in Ky.: wheat, 50 cts. on sale; corn, no sale at any price; other produce accordingly. The reason of the low price of produce [is] so secesh will not allow shipping down the r[i]ver and U.S. says can't think of letting you send your Eatables south for the support of rebbel armies.

Fruits which normally sell with no [?] at 8 cts. sells here for 20, 8 cts. mushn [mushrooms?] 20 cts., coffee 80 cts., sugar 20 cts., tea $1.25 and so on. And as [I] hav[en]'t time to write any more, my love to all the friends, a kiss to our little ones, and don't forget nor grieve for your ever devoted husband

G.W. Squier

1. "C." is unidentified other than by the context which makes it appear that he/she is a relative or friend in Indiana. "C." could be the "Charly" of the Letter 2 above or the "Charlotte" of 4 below.

Soldiers could send letters without prepaying postage. The cost of mailing the letter would be paid by the addressee. Squier's letter of July 26, 1862 (Letter 9), was such a "solder's" [sic] letter. See also Letter 4 in chapter 2. "We have a hard time to get postage stamps," wrote Pvt. William D. Groves of Company H on January 10, 1862; quoted in Robert Willey, *The Iron 44th* (n. p., n. d.), 18. (Copy of this publication was made available to the editors by Richard and Wilda Skidmore.)

LETTER 4

Calhoon [Kentucky] Feb. 5, 1862

Dear Wife,

The day after I mailed my last letter (Jan. 21), I was taken sick. Stayed in my tent for two days. Was taken to Hospital. Our regimental surgeon (which the boys call "Instent death") looked at me and said "Typhoid fever." Was pretty sick a few days. Had first rate attention from all but particularly Randy Simmons.[1] Platt stuck right by me through rough and [?] like a Dear good Brother as he is. I shal allways consider myself under obligations for the kindness and constant attention which he has given me. He went nearly two mils and paid twenty cents for a chicken for me. In fact, when I had recovered, he was entirely tired out and sick. He as well as myself are once moore nearly well and in camp and it really seems like getting home.

We left Carrollton on the 1st inst.[2] The cause of mooving back here no one knows. Our tents are pitched in the same place that we left some Sixteen days before. The weather here for two days is very fine, roads very muddy. The box of things arrived a[t] Carrollton Jan. 22. The things came in fine order, and you may believe the boys had a good time with the good things that kind friend sent so far. Your letter of the 19th ult. came to hand, I think about the 2nd or 3rd of this month. I read the letter yesterday dated Jan. 13. So you [know], I do not allways get your letters direct. It is of little use to send papers, for they are generaly [taken by?] the first hands they pass into within the lines of the encampment. I did *not* get the "Times" you sent. Am glad you have got rid of *part* of the hogs. Had you not better have the rest of them butchered? You know, *your* pork [?] is at "Jake" Warbec's.[3] Better have a well dug. You spoke of having a [?] put in. If it is not seasoned thoroughly it will make the water unfit for use for some time. If you wish to plank it up, you can get some of Hopkin's [?].[4] Should you get plank perhaps Lafayette will throw it on the waggon when he goes up home.[5] I'm glad you are going on your visit at last. Was *very, very* sory to hear Charlie is so very poorly. I do hope he will yet recover, and it seemes to me that he will. The health of the boys of Sapir[?] is generally good. Thomas Parks is dead, as you have doubtless heard.[6] It is now nearly dark and I must close. Give my love to all the friends. I have not yet rcd. a letter from Charlotte.[7] When you g[et] to Farmer, tell me whether you will have letters addressed to Farmer Center or some where else. Don't know when we shal be paid off, probably at the close of the term of our enlistment if not [before?]. I *do* feel a[n]xious to send you some money, for I know you need it. Once moore, good by. I am as ever your affectionate Husband

George

GWS

1. William W. Martin was then the regiment's surgeon. He resigned August 1, 1863. Cpl. Randall Simmons was a member of Company D. As noted above, Squier did not recover completely from this illness and was hospitalized for much of February and March. The illness troubled him for the remainder of his life.
2. Company records indicate January 31 as the date of departure from Carrollton. So did Private Groves. See *Supplement to the Official Records of the Union and Confederate Armies,* vol. 17 (Wilmington, N.C., 1994–), 262 (hereafter cited as *OR Supplement*); Willey, *Iron 44th,* 19.
3. Jake Warbec is unidentified. From the context, he seems to have been a neighbor in Indiana.
4. Hopkin is unidentified. The meaning may have been that Ellen could get the planks from a neighbor named Hopkin.

5. Lafayette was almost certainly George Squier's younger brother (1839–1916).

6. Thomas R. Parks, a member of Company D, died at Henderson, Kentucky, January 15, 1862, of typhoid pneumonia. See Rerick, *The Forty-fourth Indiana Volunteer Infantry*, 29.

7. The context of several of the letters indicates that Charlotte was a sister or sister-in-law of George or Ellen Squier. See especially Letter 11 in chapter 2.

LETTER 5

Pittsburgh, Tenn. Apr. 10th, 1862

Dear, Dear Ellen,

I have seen the "Elephant"—was in the great battle that came off on last Sunday & Monday.[1] I came through safe but our Dear poor brother was wounded very badly. A musket ball struck on the right side of the bowels and passed through the point of the hip bone. The intestines are not damaged, so say the surg[e]ons, and the only trouble with propper care is the damage done the bone. He with the rest of the Indiana boys will probably be sent to Evansville or some other point in their own state as Gov. Morton[2] is here for that purpose. I told Platt he had better write or telegraph as soon as possible after his arrival at the hospital for father to come for him as soon as he arrives. Consequently p[l]an as it will necessrily be months before he will be able for duty.

We are not allowed to write particulars about battle[s]. You will receive by the press the whole particulars long before the receipt of this. Had the ague this A.M. Do not feel very bright. Will write moore next time. Should have [written] one sooner but could not send out for mail until this time. Received yours of 27 March. Was so glad to hear that mother and all the rest of the friends were improving so finely. It is night and I am allmos[t] tried out, so good by Dear ones. Give my love to all and remember me as ever your affectionate and loving

George

1. To have "seen the elephant" meant that a soldier had had his baptism of fire—his first taste of combat. The expression originally referred to the experience of people who would do odd jobs for a visiting circus in order to be allowed to "see the elephant." The expression was often used in a context meaning that viewing the pachyderm was not worth all the work one had to do to see him or her—hence, an experience that was not as good as it was supposed to be. The reference here is to Squier's participation in the Battle of Shiloh, fought Sunday and Monday, April 6–7, 1862.

2. Oliver P. Morton, Republican governor of Indiana and a staunch supporter of the Union war effort. Like the good politician that he was, Morton took a great interest in the welfare of his state's soldiers. See Butler, *Story*, 126; Rerick, *The Forty-fourth Indiana Volunteer Infantry*, 60.

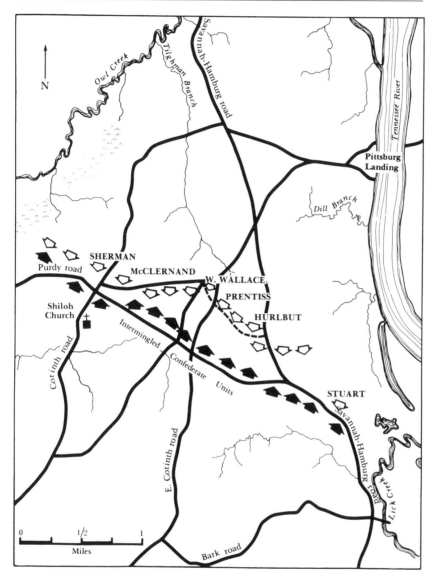

Development of the Hornets' Nest, 9–12 A.M., April 6, 1862. Map by Rudy Sanders from Shiloh—In Hell Before Night *by James Lee McDonough. Used with permission.*

LETTER 6

Pittsburgh Landing, Tenn. April 13th, 1862

Dear, Dear Ellen,

I wrote a few lines two or three days since but having a little leisure will scribble little thinking that you may want to hear from P.[Platt]. He has left here for some hospital down the river, perhaps Evansville. I do hope he will be able to send word home of his whereabouts and that Father or Lafayette will come and take him home where he will receive much better care, and if he dies he will be among friends and *at home.*

My health is now very good for me. Have found many acquaintances here in the army. The 14th Ohio, 30th Ind. regts. are here. Tell Charlotte that a gentleman whose initials are Charles Welch[1] called on me yesterday. [He] looked remarkably well and appeared to be very glad to see *not* his Brother-in-law but friend.

There just now is passed up our company the cry "mail." [I] wonder if there is a letter for me—there was your second letter to "Dixie." I'm so glad to hear from home that you appeared to be getting along so well. And O! I *am so* thankful that mother (the Dear creatu[re]) is getting along so well. Better have some garden made in due season; plant some potatoes, onions, &c&c. You make [the] garden. As I used to chop, get some one else to do it.

On Friday P.M. (4th inst), we heard cannonading, appearantly about 5 mils distant, but supposed it to be artillery practicing. At 6 ¼ P.M. long roll beat "to arms". Line of battle was formed and we marched out about 1 ½ mils when we learned that our pickets had been driven in by about two Thousand of the enemy. Imediately a brigade of infantry and battery of artillery were sent out and put the rebels to flight, with a loss on their side of about twenty killed and 9 prisoners, and of our side 3 killed and 2 prisoners with some few slightly wounded.[2]

Of course you have seen many accounts of the great battle here of last Sunday and Mon.,[3] and written by men who are accustomed to write and picture things in their true light, for let me say the scene cannot be over drawn in this case. I think you will be safe in believing the largest account as the nearest correct.

The fight (now if this "bores" you say so, or at least don't read it) commenced at 3 o'clock Sundy morning. Our pickets were driven in, and in 15 minutes the enemy were within our lines. The regiments along our lines held them in check, retreating slowly; the enemy stopping to pillage our camps. At 6 in the morning the fight became quite general; we heard the discharges of musketry and artillery and now we had a work to perform, but we little imagined the extent of that work. We examined our arms [and] filled our canteens with water, waiting for the call. Nor did we wait long. At 10 min. past 6 the long roll sounded throughout our camp and in five min. we were in line of battle on our parrade ground. As we stood there (some five minutes[)] the thought passed through my mind: of the thousands so full of life now how many will return? And strange music too for that beautiful sabbath morning was the officers passing with lightning speed and in loud voices giving commands, the rattle of Sabers and carbines, clattering of hoofs, jarring of artillery as they hurried over the rough road, the booming of a hundred cannon, and the discharge of thousands of muskets. The command was given "right face" and we moved off to the scene of action. We soon met wounded men, citizens, and women fleeing to the boats for security. We met some with the loss of fingers, some without a hand, some with a broken leg or arm; in fact, [they were] wounded in every conceivable place. I mention this because at *that* time it rather daunted my fervor and for the first time I doubted my courage.

We passed along some distanc[e] when a shell from the enemy's gun struck a tree, shivering it to pieces and bursting a little to the right of our line. We passed along and took our position. Were ordered to lay down flat on our faces. [We] lay there perhaps for nearly an hour when Col. Read[4] rode up and requested Liet. Wayne[5] (as brave a man as ever lived) to take ten men and try and discover the possiton of the enemy. He soon returned and reported the enemy advancing (we were stationed in the woods on a slight raise of ground with thick underbrush in front). We waited but a short time when the order was passed along our line "fire" and the discharge of 800 muskets broke upon the air. We lay on the ground to load, raised, and fired; we fought for nearly an hour when the enemy fled the field with tremendous loss. Our company lost one man killed and two wounded.

Right here you may wish to know how I "stood fire". I will tell you while laying on the ground and just before we reced. orders to fire I simply breathed faith: "Ever kind Father preserve me." When I arose and the firing [began I] was as cool and composed as if sitting down for a chat or shooting squirrells. The bulletts whistled over our heads, shells bursting all around us, balls whiz[zi]ng past, tearing trees, &c&c. At 10 o'clock we were again attacked, but this time they could not stand our fire more than about 40 minuts when they again fled. Col. rode up & down our lines, his face fairly shining, [and] said "boys, can you give that a cheer," and we did give three rousing cheers. A bullet passed through the Col.'s coat Sleave, also one through Platt's coat sleave and grazed his side, but did not cut through the skin. While I was laying on my face a bullet whistled over my head and passed through my Haversack.

Our position in the line of battle was about the center of the left wing of our army. Up to about 12 o'clock we were not really fighting moore than 1 ¾ hours (our regiment I mean). At 12 we were orderd to our left to support our battery. While marching along we could see scores of dead men and horses stretched on the ground. We had scarcely taken our position when A. Willson from Maysville was shot through the arm[6] and I was ordered to take him to the rear about 80 rods to a cluster of old buildings, where I bound up his arm. Scarsely was it done when Mr. Shook[7] came in in a similar condition. The first and only time during the day that I felt like dodging was in going back to our Co. through the perfect shower of bullets, grape & canister shot, shell and ball. Every few minuts I would catch myself dodging or winking to screen myself from the messengers of death that flew so thickly all around, above and in front. We had taken position on quite a raise of ground. There were few trees and no underbrush either in front or rear, and [we] were in full view of the enemy, exposed to the most deadly fire from infantry and artillery. Here is where fell many, *very* many of the brave sons of Indiana. We held our position for hours, advancing and retreating by turns until about 4 o'clock, when the ene[m]y succeded in planting a battery to our left and a little in the rear. When we were subject to a most deadly crossfire besids the fire in front, this was rather moore than even Indiana valor could withstand, and we were ordered to retreat.

Just before this Platt was wounded, and it became my duty to leave the field and take care of my brother. We hurried back through the delluge of balls. As we were passing an old rail pen, a shell fell not moore than 15 feet from us but behind the pen, and burst in a thousand pieces, scattering the fragments all around us. We found our Dr.[8] He dressed Platt's wound and ordered me to get him to the boat imediately, as our forses were gradually falling back but gallantly contesting every inch of ground they lost. I carried Platt and asisted him in walking by turns until we finally got to the landing. [I] got Platt seated, then set about looking up a place on board [the] boat. Finally succeeded and got Platt aboard and comfortably situated in a state room. It was now nearly dark. The fireing nearly ceased, but I am sorry to say, not until the enemy had possesion of the camp of the 44th. But it was not done until our men were worn out with fighting, and their ranks thined by the awfuly distructive fire under which we had fought for so many hours.

To give you an idea of how we suffered, let me tell you we Company D went on to the field 217 files of men and at 4 P.M. when I left there were only 8 files, and at 5 only 5 files or 10 men, the ballance having been killed or wounded.[9] A few of course [were] necessarily absent to take [care] of the badly wounded.

Aprl 16. I have an opportunity of sending this "out," that is, to some point wher there is a P.O. [post office], so I will close. My health is good, weather fair and cool. We shall probably have another fight within a few days at Corinth, some twenty mils from this place. The rebbels are in strong force there and must be driven out.

Tell Sister C.[10] [I] Should like to hear from her as often as convenient. Give my love to mother & Father. Tell them they need not look for me home until this rebellion is crushed out and our beloved Country once moore free, unless [I am] disabled by sickness or otherwise. My love to all the friends and especially to our little folks. So good by Dear one and believe me as ever your affectionate

George

Tell Cyrene[11] I'm glad he's home safe and sound. Hope he will not have to come back though I should like to see him very much.

G.

1. Charles Welch is unidentified except by context. He was not a member of the 14th Ohio or the 30th Indiana. If he was a soldier, he may have been Pvt. Charles Welch of Com-

pany K, 1st Ohio Cavalry, who enlisted on September 22, 1861. He later became a sergeant and was mustered out with the regiment on September 13, 1865. The regiment was
part of the reinforcements that reached the army at Shiloh. *Official Roster of the Soldiers
of the State of Ohio in the War of the Rebellion, 1861–1865,* vol. 11 (Akron, 1888), 4, 41.

2. This affair—typical of many that summer—was so insignificant that no mention of it
appears in U.S. War Department, comp., *The War of the Rebellion: Official Records of the
Union and Confederate Armies* (Washington, 1880–1902) (hereafter cited as *OR,* with all
references to volumes in series 1) or in the *OR Supplement.* See the excerpt from Groves's
letter of May 11, 1862, in Wiley, *Iron 44th,* 51–52.

3. The Battle of Shiloh April 6–7, 1862. For a general account, see Wiley Sword, *Shiloh:
Bloody April* (Dayton, Ohio, 1983). The battle opened on the morning of April 6 when
the Confederates made a surprise attack on the Federal camps in the area around Pittsburg
Landing. At that time, the 44th Indiana was camped with its division (Maj. Gen. Stephen
R. Hurlbut's) near the rear of the Union position. As Squier indicates, the regiment moved
into the fight and was engaged near the famous Peach Orchard. After taking heavy losses—
but playing an important part in delaying the Confederate advance—the division fell back
to the "last line" near the landing where the Federals held. From that position on the
morning of April 7, the reinforced Unionists attacked and drove the Southerners from
the field.

4. Col. Hugh B. Reed of Fort Wayne commanded the regiment until he resigned on November 26, 1862.

5. Lt. Charles H. Wayne of Maysville and Company D. He commanded the company April
6–7 at Shiloh after Capt. Franklin B. Cosgrove was badly wounded early in the battle.

6. Alfred Wilson, whose residence is listed in the roster as Harlan. In December 1862 he
was one of the men transferred to the "Regulars" (see Letter 16).

7. Joseph and Lewis Shook were both members of Company D. The latter died January
10, 1863; the former was discharged April 29, 1863, for disability.

8. Probably Martin (see Letter 4, note 1), but he could have been John H. Rerick, then assistant surgeon of the regiment, later surgeon, and, later still, author of the regiment's
history.

9. Squier certainly meant "217 files of men" in the regiment, not the company. A file was a
group of men lined up one behind another. The regiment's strength at the beginning of
the battle was 478. Deducting officers, there would have been about 434 enlisted men
for the battle and, if the regiment was deployed in the common formation of two lines,
about 217 files would be correct for the regiment. Colonel Reed's report of the regiment's
role in the battle is in *OR,* vol. 10, pt. 1, 238–40. Squier's concluding installment on the
Battle of Shiloh is in Letter 10.

10. Possibly Charlotte. See Letter 4, note 7.

11. Cyrenus Saunders of Hall's Corners, a member of Company D, who was then at home
in Indiana. He later returned to the regiment and served until discharged on March 23,
1863. See Letter 14 in this chapter and Letter 8 in chapter 2.

LETTER 7

Near Pittsburgh Landing, Tenn. Apr. 25th, 1862

Ever Dear Ellen,

Yesterday we struck tents and marched about three mils. in a South Westerly direction, about 3 mils from our old camping ground. We are now encamped in a very pretty oak grove with a small clear streem running in front. The water is not as good as at our old "home," but the woods and flowers make amends for that. You know I am quite fond of flowers. Is it not very kind in our Father to furnish us with so many sourses of enjoyment? Though deprived of the society of Dear friends [and] seperated from all I hold most Dear on Earth, yet I find great comfort in roving through the woods among strang[e] plants and flowers. I can see a beauty in nature now that I never saw before, can trace the hand [of] an allwise Providence who is ever kind and indulgent. There [I] must stop and help get dinner.

Oh dear! Oh dear! It has been fourteen days since Platt left and yet no word from him. Have watched lists of the wounded arriving at different hospitals appearing in the papers but not one word can I find about the 44th. Oh! If I could only know of his whereabouts and whether he is still alive it would be such a relief. It seems that I could endure anything better than this awful suspence. There has been but very little mail for the regt. for several days. It seems to be my fate to have no mail when I feel that I must hear from some of my friends. You know that was the case when mother was sick. Dr. Rerick our ast. surgon (I can spell surgeon) received a letter from a friend of P.'s enquiring where he had been sent.

I have recd. a letter from home sinc[e] your no. 3—have written one since that. There has been some alteration in our position in the army since my last. Our brigade now consists of the 11th & 26th Ky, 13th Ohio, & 44 Ind. regts. commanded by Gen. Critenden[1] in Maj. Gen. Buel's Division.[2] It is said that we will be held in reserve but that is uncertain.[3] We are now encamped near the 30th Ind. in which are several boys of my acquaintans, Robbert Murphy[4] among the number. There is doubtless many of the 44th boys at home as I understand that all the wounded that were able were sent home. What would I not give to know that Platt was among the number. But of cours he is not unless Father came after him. He is hardly out of my mind during the day, and often, very often do I send up a silent petition for his preservation and restoration to his friends. And when I lay down at night I never forget to ask our Allmighty Father to keep him in his kind care. It is truly a good thing to have some one to whom we can tell all our troubles and trials, one who was "tempted in all things like as we ar[e]" and one who is *not* unwilling to hear and "help in every time of need."[5] The thought often passes through my mind—what Infinite Goodness, what Infinite goodness to poor erring mankind.

It is allmost dark and I must "qu[i]t." O yes, Mr. Bayless (Father knows him) is in camp.[6] He will return to Fort Wayne in a few days (probably not until after the fight comes off at Corinth),[7] and I with many others intend sending our money by him. Tell Wilber, Allice and Ella that I send each of them a kiss right here ————. Give my love to all the friends and especially to our Dear, Dear mother. And now Dear Ellen, good night and may Heaven bless and protect you is the prayer of your un-worthy but ever loving and affectionate

George

Do you remember *that* eveneing we spent in our (yors I mean) front room at the West window some six months since? I do and often very often think of it. Shal *we* ever sit there again? Let us hope for the best. Would it not be very pleasant? But "PShaw," why do I think of the past, much less write it. And the future now seldom troubls me, but sometimes I will catch myself making some calculations. But here I *must* bid you one moore good by.

George W. S.

Tell Sister Hortense[8] I'd like very much to see her and eat *that* pickle she promised me. We can get them here though for only five cents apiece now. I [would] like to here from her and Lafayette "Wall."[9] I would like to see that awful Nephew *and hear it cry.* It's been rainny all day and still it rains. My health is good. Army fare and "Sunny South" appears to agree with my health. O yes, I said it was dark some time sinc[e] but it is now candle light.

G.W. Squier

1. In April and May 1862, the Federal forces that had fought at Shiloh underwent a bewil-dering series of reorganizations. When all was said and done, the 44th Indiana had been returned to the Army of the Ohio and assigned to Brig. Gen. (later Maj. Gen.) Thomas L. Crittenden's division. The brigade commander was Brig. Gen. Horatio P. Van Cleve.
2. Maj. Gen. Don Carlos Buell commanded the "Center" of the force that advanced from Shiloh to Corinth in April and May 1862. Later he commanded the Army of the Ohio, which in June 1862 was sent to operate in north Alabama and central Tennessee. This army became the Army of the Cumberland.
3. Crittenden's division was assigned to the army reserve, but it operated under Buell's com-mand.
4. Murphy, from Allen County, enlisted in Company E, 30th Indiana, September 24, 1861. He transferred to the Marine Brigade (a force operating with the Union navy on the Mis-sissippi River) on March 14, 1863.
5. This quotation seems to derive from Hebrews 4:15–16, although the wording is not exact.
6. Unidentified except as in the text. The context makes it clear that he was a family friend visiting the army. Perhaps he was an agent for the U.S. Sanitary Commission. See Letter 11, chapter 2.
7. After Shiloh, the massive Federal army advanced slowly southwest toward Corinth, Mis-

sissippi, twenty miles away. The Yankees expected the Confederates to make a stand at Corinth because of the town's importance as a railroad center, but the Rebels evacuated it at the end of May without a fight.

8. Sister Hortense is unidentified except by the context, which makes it clear she was a sister or sister-in-law of George or Ellen Squier.

9. The context makes it clear that this is a reference to Lafayette Squier's son. See Letter 4, note 5.

LETTER 8

Camp 8 Miles from Corrint [Corinth] May 8th, 1862

My own Dear Ellen,

I received yours of 23 ult. [and] 3 inst. which contain the awful though not entirely unlooked for intelligence of Platt's death. I have time to write but very little. In fa[c]t I hesitated about writing until after the[. . . .] I have been sick or rather decidedly grunting for several days. Have not been able to eat anything but light soups since Saturday now. But am better to day.

Write often. Should [I] fall in the coming battl I trust we shal meet [in that] haven of sweet repose where parting is no moore. I do feel qu[i]te a[n]xious about our dear little ones. But all I can do is commit you all to the <care of?> that Being who is ever kind to his children.

I must close, for we have been held "ready to march at a moment's warning" for three hours, and this is the last opportunity we shal have for some time of sending letters. Write whether you got the money $55 I sent you in care of Watson Well,[1] Fort Wayne, addressed to Father. Good by dear one and may heaven bless and preserve you is the prayer of your own

George

1. Watson Well is unidentified except by context, which makes it clear he was a relative or friend in Fort Wayne.

LETTER 9

Camp Near Battle Creek, Tenn. July 26th, 1862

My own Dear Ellen,

And stil no tidings from home since the first of the month, which may be easily accounted for as R.R. [railroad] track is being torn up, bridges burned, and *we are living on half rations.*[1] You doubtles think this hard or rather short fare. Not so. We live so far quite as well as we have sinc[e] we left Evansville. Our rations or half rations are now 6 oz. "Sow belly," 8 oz. hard bread, ¼ Gill beans or peas, ½ oz. coffee,

1 oz. Sugar per day. This seems like "small allowance," but you will remember we are in the rich valley of the Tenn. and near Battle creek, where grow hogs, Sheep, Steers, potatoes, apples, &c&c. And the boy[s] of Indiana are not going to be stinted where they are to be found *in an enemies country,* where 9/10 of the holders of property are to day in the ranks of the enemy, giving him imme[n]se power, if indeed numbers constitut[e] power. There is but little pilfereing or little petty "snouging" going on. It is done in rather a whol[e]sal[e] way. For instance, 3 days sin[ce] an officer with 75 men and on[e] team went out in the morning, [and] came in the afternoon with 2 beeves, 6 hogs, 10 bush. apples, and various other things to[o] numerous to mention. To day Lieut. Wayne is out with 2 teams and 40 men. What is taken from union men is liberally paid for, but we [do] business "on time" with secesh.[2]

My health is *very* good, better than for this season of the year for 15 years. Weather for a few days past rather cool, with very cooll nights. In past nights universally cooller here than further north as far as my experience goes.

I wrote to our little fo[l]ks, directed to A.W.[3] Have you rcd. $5 sent pr. mail from near Tuscumbia? Also $20 in care of Watson Well. I do not k[n]ow whether my letters go through or not. Have you hea[r]d from the first money I sent? If not had you not better write to Westly Park,[4] Auburn, Dekalb Co., Ind. He left us at Florenc[e] for home. [He] said he would endeavor to find it on his return home.

You may think [it] strange I do not write moore. Have been very busy in "straigtning up" Co. arrears. Our capt.[5] (think a wooden man would do as well) made out papers [only] for a single Deceased soldier. Consequently the[re] has been an amo[u]nt of writing to do, which is the duty of the Co. commander, but I have done the most of the writing since June 1st, which keeps me rather busy. Lieut. Reas[6] starts home tomorrow morning. I send this by him to some [post] office. Write often and do not I bessech expect letters regularly as it is impossable to sent them, mail communication being of very often cut off. While we lay in camp I shal write as often as one a week, whether you get them or not.

Good by loved one and may Heaven's choicest blessings rest on you and our dear, *Dear* little ones is ever the prayer of you[r] own

George

Cyrene and Bert[7] are "all right." Co. D goes on out-post duty tonight. No reliable news from Richmond. Guerilla parties are doing much damage in this state and Ky.

G.W.S.

Out of <?> stamps. Consequently mak[e] solder's letter.
Address: Crittenden's Division, Buel's Army via Nashville

1. After the capture of Corinth, the 44th Indiana moved with its division and the rest of
   Buell's army eastward toward Chattanooga. From late May to August, Company D was
   stationed in the Manchester-Jasper-Bridgeport area. That summer, Confederate raiders

often disrupted Federal plans by wrecking railroads that would have supplied the invading Yankees. Many Northern units were diverted from other operations to guard the lines of supply.

2. The regiment gained a reputation for ignoring orders to protect the property of civilians. Colonel Reed once told General Buell of "the folly of expecting men with guns in their hands to resist such temptation, when living on half rations of 'sow belly' [pork] and 'hardtack' [army bread]." See Letter 14 below and Letter 2 in chapter 2. See also the comments in Willey, *Iron 44th*, 56–60, 64–66; Butler, *Story*, 163, 166–73; and Rerick, *The Forty-fourth Indiana Volunteer Infantry*, 101–3.

3. "A. W." is unidentified. The context makes it clear that he or she was a relative or friend in Indiana.

4. Wesley Park was captain of Company K until he resigned on December 10, 1861. From Squier's comments, it is clear that he remained with or returned to the regiment after he resigned—perhaps awaiting approval of the paperwork.

5. The captain was Franklin K. Cosgrove of Harlan, who resigned September 3, 1862.

6. Probably 1st Lt. Elias D. Rose of Company A, whose resignation was effective July 22, 1862. Pvt. Robert D. Rhea of Company D was discharged July 31, 1862.

7. Bert was probably Albert Jackson of Hall's Corners, a member of Company D.

LETTER 10

Camp near Battle Creek, Tenn. July 30, 1862

Dear Ellen,

Though I have written so often since we came to this camp, I will venture a few lines, but really hardly know what to write as there is no excitement, nothing to break the dull monotony of camp life. O! Yes, there has been one of those awful rain storms for an hour past which completely flooded the tents, which made it qu[i]te unpleas[an]t for me, but the boys enjoyed it amazingly. Peeping out of the doore, I saw numberless "bodies" in "all thier native purity" runn[in]g, jumping, wrestleing, in fact "cutting all sorts of didoes."

Perhaps I may have time now to finish "Shiloh," though it has been so long since you will not expe[c]t much (you know my memory). Well, to commen[ce]. If I mistake not I left our troops retreating bak towards the river. They fell back 1 ½ mils. from our first position, where were found the broken and scattered fragment of the regiments. Formed on hill decidedly to our advantage, resolved to hold our position or die. Again was herd the crack of the musket, the whistleing and deadly bullet, bursting of shell, the cries of the wounded, the thunder of our large seige guns and the 120 pounders from the gun boats, which dealt death and distruction to the vile hord[e] which came so near [to] overpowering the hard handfull of men opposing them. We had at this time not moore than 1000 men who had been fighting all day with nothing to eat, not a moment's rest, but little water (no one knows how the pangs of thirst in battle but he who has e[x]perienced it)—but men who would rather die than yield. The fight continued until night parted the combattents, when we had suceeded in driving the rebbels back near ¾ of a mile in this fight which lasted about ten hours. Desperate as it was, the 44th's loss was but triffling. Co. D lost not a man.

I have noticed in some of the journals of the day statements that Gen. Grant's army were completely routed, demoralized, and on the point of falling into the hands of the enemy.[1] But that is false. We were not "whipped," though driven back, being unable to hold so long a line against more than three times our number. The position occupied on sundy evening, 5 o'clock could and *would* have been held for another day without reinforcements, but of course must have been eventually overpowerd by the vastly superior numbers of the ene[m]y had we not been reinforced. Thes[e] statements were made either by wounded men who were completely unmande[d] by the pain they endured and imagined the thing much wors than it was, by cowerds who left their comrads to face the danger and win or loose the battle as they could and themselves take refuge beneath the riverbank, or by men who wished to detra[c]t from Grant's army. Many of the letter[s] were from *our sister state* Ohio (they doubtless felt mortified at the disgracef[ul] conduct of some of their troops).

But then to the battle—night finaly put an end to the deadly strif[e], to that awful Sabbeth's day's work. We lay on our armes withou[t] blankets or food while the rain poured down in torrents for nearly half the night. An awful night was that one. Could amid the roar of the thunder hear the groans of the wounded & dying, and ever and anon might be heard above every thing else the report of the guns on the "Tyler."[2] Walking in the dark one would perhaps stumble over some poor victim of the deadly bullet who lay cold and stiff in death, or some wounded and dying fellow who thus roused from his death stupor would call for help, perhaps for water.

But why think of those scens of terror, pain and death? The night wore away. Another day dawned, another day of strife, of labor, pain, blood and death, *and of victory. B[r]eakfasted on raw pork* & hard bread. Called into [line] about 7 A.M. and mooved to the front and left of the line. Took position on slight rais of ground to the right of a battery which was play[ing] with great effe[c]t on the enemy. But scarsely had we (the 44th and 31st) formed in line of battl[e] when the enemy appeerd, coming over the hill in front in close column double quick, with fixed bayonets, determ[in]ed to take the guns which so much annoyed them. Three times the order *"fire low"* passed along the lines and simultaneous was heerd the crack of 300 muskets. Three hundred bullets were hurled on their death errand. Each time did their ranks thin and waver, but on they came [to] capture t[he] guns, carriages, cassons & horses. Again the word "Fire" passed along the line—then "fix Bayonets" [and] Charge bayonets. And on we dashed and [in] less than five minits the battery was retaken with several prisoners. The fight continued. Sometimes we were advancing, sometimes retreeting until about 4 P.M. when the rout of the enemy became general. Co. D was very fortin[ate] on this day's fight, as we did [not] loose a man.[3]

I might have been more minute in details but it is anything but plesant to recall individual scens, scenes which one *cannot* forget though he would. I have not time to read this scrawl and make corrections. I know it is awfully written but am in a hurry. Good by dear one and remember me to all, especially to our little ones and Mother.

George

Address: 44th Ind. vol.
Critenden's Brigade

1. Maj. Gen. (later Lt. Gen.) Ulysses S. Grant commanded the Union forces that fought at Shiloh. His army was surprised but not routed and demoralized on the first day of that battle. Reinforcements received during the night of April 6–7 enabled him to drive the Confederates away. Later he would command the Federal troops who captured Vicksburg and then those who secured the Unionists' hold on east Tennessee. In the spring of 1864, Grant was named overall commander of the Northern armies and directed them in the last year of the war. He was president of the United States 1869–77.

2. *Tyler* was a Union gunboat. She and *Lexington* lay in the Tennessee River firing at the Confederates through the night of April 6–7.

3. No separate official report of casualties in Company D on April 7 has surfaced. Surgeon Rerick gave the company's loss in the two-day battle as six killed or mortally wounded and seventeen wounded (*The Forty-fourth Indiana Volunteer Infantry,* 57). Reed reported that the battle cost the regiment 34 killed, 177 wounded, and 1 captured. Later, the figures were revised to 24 killed and 174 wounded. *OR,* vol. 10, pt. 1, 103, 240.

LETTER II

Indianapolis Nov. 6, 1862[1]

Dear Ellen,

And yet we are here on expence and in suspence waiting, waiting for men to do an hour's work. But money is the order of the day. Little difference how it is made, whethe[r] it be defrauding the Government or the private soldier who leaves his family and friends, sunders tender ties, sacrifices his little means for the good of his country. I tell you when I see the deception, the low dispisable cunning used to gain position and profit, I have to clentch my hands to prevent my patriotism coming out at the ends of my fingers. I can hardly feell like cursing this government, but the way the affairs of this nation is conducted—merit is not respected; a man's rights is not recognisced; men are dogs. Shoulder straps and money are *Deities*—they rule this nation. And O how! I have but littl hop[e]s of closing this awful war until the day comes that there is no money to be made—when the credit of the country is lost. Then perhaps men may take time to turn their attention to the true interest of the Goverment. I wish that to day Govement Scrip was not worth 20 cts. on the Dollar, but [as] it is fortuns are being made every day. Money is plenty but the day is comeing for this to end. Would that it was now. But reelly this is faultfinding—this is treason and I must stop.

I beli[e]ve I wrote you that I could not possably send you more than $50, perhaps not that [if] we do not get our clothing act. [account] settled on which there is due me $14.50. Instead of getting Regulation price (75 cts. pr. day) for subsistanc[e], we got 30 cts., which mak[e]s qu[i]te a differenc as you may perceive. Instead of getting $100 I get $63. I bought me a vest, a pr. of Gloves, some papers and envelops, a po[r]t folio, a tooth brush, a knife, and some such littl notions that I really needed or *thought* I did. I some times feell rather conscience-smitten that I have paid out so much money for my self for things I *could* get along without, when I consider how much I am oweing. I have not yet got me a rubber blanket. Don't know whether I shal chance gett[in]g one at the Regt. or not.

No[w] Ellen do not pay out all the money on those debts, for I probably shal not d[r]aw [pay] again for several months in all probability. Tell dear little Ella that pa did not entirely forget her under sleaves, and Allice—the dear loving creature—I thought she must have some as nic[e]. O! Yes—how did Charlotte and Lomira[2] get along that day? I would like to have them write often if they can. One who has never been long from home has no idea of the feelling on the recept of letters from friends.

Lieut. *Wayne and lady* left this place this mo[rni]ng. Yes, "Charly" is married. [I] like the appearance of the lady very much. Perfect lady in appearance—kind, courteous, and affection[at]e. I should thi[n]k her just the one I could wish a friend to marry. Spent some time in her company. Went dow[n] to the Depot with them. She took down your address, intending to write. We *kissed* and parted. After an acquance of a few hours it now seems that we have been acquainted for years. Charlie is sick and cannot rejoin his Co. for some time. He is very a[n]xious I should get to the regt. as soon as possabl and take command of the Co., as Lieut. Shell is sick.[3] Give my love to all—Father, Mother, Brother, & Sisters. A kiss for our Dear little ones and love to your own Dear self.

George

Tuesday, Oct. [Nov.] 11

I've been here hard at work for nearly two weeks doing Nothing. I am well but have sore Eyes. Write often.

George

Canot conjecture when we may leave for the Regt.

1. Squier's presence in Indianapolis may have resulted from another bout with illness and a medical furlough or from his being selected for recruiting services. In the late summer of 1862, one officer and one enlisted man from each company of the regiment returned to Indiana to raise replacements for men who had been killed in action or lost to wounds or disease. See Willey, *Iron 44th*, 61. How long these detached officers and men were on duty at home is unknown.

    Whatever the reason for his trip to Indiana, Squier had a chance to visit with Ellen at home and in Indianapolis that fall (see Letter 3, chapter 4). He seems to have left to re-

Capt. George Shell of Company D, 44th Indiana Volunteer Infantry. Courtesy of Bob Willey.

join the regiment about October 15 (see Letter 15). Squier missed all or part of the Kentucky Campaign and the Battle of Perryville fought on October 8. By the time he rejoined the regiment, it was back in middle Tennessee.

2. Lomira is unidentified. She was probably a sister or sister-in-law of George or Ellen Squier. She may be the person referred to as "L" in Letter 14. See also Letters 4 and 11, chapter 2.

3. 2d Lt. (later Capt.) George W. Shell of Hall's Corners and Company D. He was promoted for gallantry at Shiloh. Shell remained with the regiment until his term of service expired on January 28, 1865.

LETTER 12

Camp Near Nashville, Tenn. Nov. 27th, 1862

Dear Wife,

We left camp on Stone river [at] 9 A.M. yesterday. Marched 9 mils. over good roads and through fine country. [There were] large plantations on either side of road with hills looming up in [the] distanc. Decidedly pleasant march. Camped on hill about two mils. S.E. from Nashville. Imediately in front we see the three large forts built within the three past months, very strong and have complete command of all the surrounding country for mils.[1] A little to the right is Nashvill with its shaded streets, its church spires, and above all the state house—the best in the west, built entirely of stone and Iron. Still farther to the right we see Mt. Olivet cemetery with its pollished marble Steps and monuments, interspeced with innumerable evergreens. Also the Cumberland river winds its course down through the hills, which make splendid scenery.

It is now one month sinc I left home, and no letter. I hardly know why as others from that Neighborhood get mail very regulerly. Perhaps my turn may come by & by.

The weather is fine with cold nights. I must close. Good by Dear one. My love to all the friends in general and to Mother, P. & S. in particuler.[2] A kiss to our little one.

G.W. Squier

1. After the Federals occupied Nashville in February 1862, they turned the city into a strongly fortified base.
2. "Mother, P. & S." is a reference to Ellen's mother ("P") and his own mother ("S")—Powers and Squier. It is clear from Letter 2 in chapter 2 that both Squier's mother and mother-in-law were living near Ellen.

LETTER 13

Camp 6 miles S.E. from Nashville, Tenn. Dec. 4th, '62

Dear Ellen,

We are yet in camp but have had a little to break the usual monotony of camp life. On Monday we had Grand Review, Genrls. Debility Critenden and Rosencrans[1] being present. We formed on large field, our whole division (5th) in line of battle, open ranks. The Genrls. rode down the whole length of the line, speaking kin[d]ly words as he (Rosencrans) passed—is very common in appearanc[e], dress plain and rather homely. So that day passed off rather well.

And yesterday the 13th Ohio and 44 were detailed to guard a forraging [train] going out on the Nashville and Murpheysborough road. The train consisted of some 40 or 50 waggons. We marched out some Four miles from camp, where our advance came in contact with the rebel viderts—fired into them and they "scedadled." We passed along with little interuption except an occasional exchange of shots, by which the rebbels lost Three men killed and two wounded. When out 8 mils. from camp we were met by about 100 rebbels—saw them comeing. We squared around and at the distance of some 50 yards the command "ready" passed along in an instent. The click of One Hundred and Fifty muskets might have been heard in another instent. The leaden mesengers would have been hurled full in the enemy's face had they not just then hoisted the white "rag." Then the command came "recover armes." The order was obeyed but a murmur of disappointment might have been heard through the whole length of our lines. A capt. bearing the flag of truce met Maj. Worthy[2] (who had charge of our train). [The captain] stated that they like ourselves were forraging and proposed that we prossed [proceed] without either party disturbing the other, and that the Maj. call in his skirmishers. He allso delivered despatches for Gen. Rosencrans. Maj. did not see fit to call in his skirmishers, and it was well that he did not for it was soon discovered that they were mooving a considerable force round to our left, evidently calculating to get in our rear and thereby cut off our retreat and capture our little squad during the daly [delay] with the flag of truce and other movements. The rebbels had sent back for reinforcements and Two sections of artillery. Our officer saw the moovement and we were ordered to fall back under cover of a slight raise of ground. We were marching by the right flank (O! yes—you may not understand all military termes so I will say in Four ranks) when the order came "file right—doble quick march." Scarcely had we got in possition when whiz went a six pound shell a few inches over your "humble servant's" head. When we were ordered to lay flat on our faces, they fired several shots over our heads but fortunately done no damage.

Had we remained in the road one minute longer we should have recieved a raking shot through our whole line, which would have mowed us down by scores. Our trains were soon loaded and mooved back. Soon we were ordered to take our back track, having accomplished our object—getting a large quantity of corn and hay. We kept up an irregular fire with the enemy's advance for several miles. We would halt every little while and give them a slight turn, not wishing to be hurried off. Had orders not to bring on an engagement, but only to defend the train. The boys did not feel satisfied but were wo[r]king under orders, and we had to return without "much fight." Our loss was one man and one Lieut. killed and one man wounded. It seems rather strange that one would [be] a[n]xious to get into a "brush," but so it is. At a distance a man dreds the idea of putting himself up for a mark, but come to the test there is something *rather* exciting in shooting, and perticulerly at one's fellow beings.[3]

To day we are on picket. The weather is fine, with cold nights. Health good. No prospects of a fight. Have receivd your two fi[r]st letters and one written at Newville in August, so you perceive letters do not allways come through overly quick. It is allmost entirely dark so good night.

Dec. 5th. Commenced snowing qu[i]te early this morn[in]g. Made it rather disagreeable but it is not cold. We were relieved about 9 A.M. It is now after noon, clear and pleasant and the snow has disappeared. Lieut. Wayne came to camp to day (he is now in hospitel at Nashville) and brought Ten loaves of bread. Fortunetely we had just drawn beef, so we had quite a feest—soft bread and Steak. Our usual fare is hard bread, "sow belly," [pork] and coffee. Troops have been stationed here so long that there is little chance of "pressing" the good things of this life.[4]

My health is good. I *did* get a testament but have but little time to read. Have a great deal of duty to perform. Has Mrs. Lieut. Wayne written to you? O! Yes, I told Charly that you rather felt disposed to "burn" me for "falling in love" with his wife. He said that my "affection was reciprocated" and proposed an even exchange. But enough—your likeness that I have gets a good ma[n]y compliments. The "boys" wonder how I happened to get so good looking a woman.

I must close, so good by Dear wife, and may Heaven bless and p[r]eserv you and our dear little ones. My love to all the fr[i]ends. Would like to hear from the sisters and brother if convenient. Think you will soon do to enlist, if you can pull trigger [on] a man in the dark.[5] Write often. Did you get the money I sent from Indianapolis, and did you receive the letter I wrote from Michelville? Good by.

George

1. Maj. Gen. William S. Rosecrans (often spelled "Rosencrans[z]" by soldiers) had replaced Buell as commander of what was now designated the Army of the Cumberland. Rerick wrote that when Rosecrans reviewed the regiment, "He made a most favorable impression on all officers and men." Rerick letter, n.d., quoted in Willey, *Iron 44th*, 74. Rosecrans led the army from October 30, 1862, to October 20, 1863, when he was removed from command after his defeat at Chickamauga. For Squier's later evaluation of "Debility Crittenden," see Letters 14 and 18 in chapter 2.
2. Major Worthy is unidentified. He was not with the 44th Indiana. Squier may have mistaken the officer's name and/or grade.
3. Attacks and skirmishes such as this were common in mid-Tennessee from the fall of 1862 to the late summer of 1863. In most cases, no reports of them appeared in *OR*. See Rerick, *The Forty-fourth Indiana Volunteer Infantry*, 77, and the December 11, 1862, letter from "A VOLUNTEER" quoted in Willey, *Iron 44th*, 75.
4. "Pressing" was soldier jargon for "impressing," or taking, goods from civilians for military use.
5. See Letters 8 and 11, chapter 2.

LETTER 14

Camp, 6 miles S.E. from Nashville, Tenn. Dec. 8th, '62

Dear Ellen,

I have written so often lately it seems rather foolish to write now but then I have nothing else to do so I will scribble a few lines. <It is> not because I get so many letters from home that I write often for I have received but two letters written since I left, two mailed in Aug.

Well, we are on picket again and I suppose tomorrow we guard forraging train. For the past Ten days we have been on duty Two days out of Three. While on picket duty I have little to do, so I usually write on such occesions. The boys find some fault with having so much duty to do, hardly having time to wash their clothes. Yesterdy

(Sundy) I washed all of my underclothes, also that shirt for the first time. And though I had worn it over a month it did not appe[a]r much dirty. I followed your instructions and did not use the washboard. Think it will not be necessary to wash them oftener than once a month.

I have drawn an overcoat because I found [it] necessary for comfort and perhaps health. When I was at Nashville got my boots half soled, which cost only $1.50. Boots are worth from $10 to $25, coffee 75 cts., sugar 40 cts., and other things in proportion. The army here is *not* well provided for, being very short of underclothes and blankets. In our Camps there are but few who have either drawers or undershirts, and some have no socks, while we have but one tent besides Headqu[a]rters, so in stormy weather the boys suffer very much. We have been in daily expectation of getting a supply of all these thi[n]gs for some time, but as yet they have not made their appearance.

Last night the sick were all sent to Nashville and we were ordered to have three days rations in H[aver] sacks and hold our selves in readiness to march at a moment's warning. The prospects are now that you will hear of lively times in Tennessee before long. What will be the result of cours the future only can disclose. It is reported here that Richmond is being evacuated.[1] If that be so the western army will have something to do. Let them come. They will, I think, meet with a warm reception.

9th. Was relieved from piket about 3 P.M. The weather is very fine, warm days and cold nights. To day we drew 3 blankets, 9 prs. socks, & 17 prs. cotton [d]rawers which was divided out to the most needy.

<I> saw Bert Jakson to day. He is well as are <the> boys generally—Cyrene, Mr. Kessler,[2] John Casebeer,[3] Tip Perkins[4] and all the rest. The 44th still keeps its name good for being a hard set of boys. A few days since an artilleryman riding by inquired what regt.—was told—said he "that d—d noisy regt. is it." Gen. Van Cleave went to Gen. Critenden with his complaints about the 44th. [He] said he could do nothing with it; they would steel every thing they could reach, go out on picket and they would take off their boots and cartridge boxes and go to sleep, &c&c. Gen. C. told him that fragment of a regt. as it is he would rather have than any other regt. in the brigade. Not long since Gen. Debility (alias Van Cleave) was riding along (this he was telling Critenden), came up to the 13th Ohio, and saw them dressing a hog as they were marching. [He] came up to the 44th, saw them skin, dress, cut up and put in their H[aver] sacks a sheep without loosing step. But I must close. My eyes are quite sore and are very tired.

Nov. [Dec.] 10. Am well. My eyes are a little better. Expect to moove in some direction, don't know where. And yet I get but one letter. It certainly seems strange. Do you write regularly! There is mail for the Regt. every day but not for *me*. Yet <I> know you write every week. As soon as my eyes are a litt<le be>tter I must write to sister C. and L.[5] We get but litt<le> news from the east. There is scarsely a day passes without a ski[r]mish in some Division of Critenden's Corps.[6]

Good by and may the day come and soon when I shal once moore [see] those lov-

*Sgt. John E. Casebeer of Company D, 44th Indiana Volun-
teer Infantry. Courtesy of Allen County–Fort Wayne Historical Society.*

ing faces. My love to all. Tell Wilber to be a good boy and dilligent in school. A kiss
for all and remember me as ever your loving Husband

G.W. Squier

For Ann Saunders:[7]

Her letter was duly received. In reffere[n]ce to Allice[8] she can do as she thinks best.
It will undoubtly cost a goodeal to keep her where she is, but if nothing better can
be done with her she of cours must remain. Perhaps it would be agreeable under the
circumstances to bring her home, but of cours he leaves it to herself. Cyrene will be
satisfied with any action she may take in the matter. He wrote a few days since. He
sends his love to Jo[9] and Eliza.[10] Wants Ann to write often and tell Jo to write. Love
to Father and mother and all the rest.

From Cyrene Saunders

1. The report was false.

2. Henry and Martin H. Kessler ("Kesler" in some records) of Hall's Corners were both privates in Company D. The former deserted on July 22, 1863; the latter served out his three-
   year term.

3. John Casebeer of Harlan, then a private in Company D, was promoted to second lieutenant in February 1865 and mustered out with the regiment.

4. Probably Lafayette Perkins, a sergeant in Company D who was from Hall's Corners and
   who served his full three-year enlistment.

5. "L." may have been Lomira. See Letter 11.

6. At this time, the larger segments of the army were called "wings." Crittenden commanded
   the "Left Wing." Informally, the wings were often called "corps." In January 1863, the
   U. S. Army formally adopted the corps organization, and it was implemented early in
   February. Crittenden's wing became the XXI Corps. The 44th Indiana was part of the
   2d Brigade, 3d Division, Crittenden's left wing. Van Cleve commanded the division; Col.
   James P. Fyffe the brigade.

7. This little section reads as if Squier wrote it for Cyrenus Saunders, who may have been
   injured or illiterate or who may have just asked Squier to have Ellen pass a message to
   Ann. See Letter 6, note 11.

8. Allice is unidentified other than by context, which makes it appear that she was a young
   girl (daughter? sister?) of Cyrenus and/or Ann Saunders.

9. Jo is unidentified except by context.

10. Eliza is unidentified except by context.

LETTER 15

Camp 4 miles S.E. from Nashville, Tenn. Dec. 15th, 1862

Dear wife,

It is a warm pleasant afternoon and [I am] feeling rather desolate amid the Supreme
noise and bustle of camp. Will scribble a few lines to let you know that I am still
alive (as I have *only averaged* about *three letters pr. week* since I left home), and have
received all of two. It is very lonely to write day after day and even weeks pass and
hear nothing from home, from loved ones. Those who have never been long absent
know not the full meaning of those three little words, "home" and "loved ones." They
know not the anxi[e]ty with which the arrival of the mail is awaited, nor the disappointment felt when one knows that he must wait at least another day and perhaps
many days more before he can hear from those who are moore dear than all things
beside on Earth. It has now been near two months since I left Halls Corners and have
received but two letters from you (except those two written in August), and none
from any one else. But then I know you all have your various home duties to attend
to and perhaps have little time for writing.

16th. Thank fortune I did not have time to finish this scrawl yesterday, and I feel
much better now as I received your very kind letter of the 10th inst. last night, in

which was Sister C.'s letter of Nov. 29th. We have had rather a hard night for men who have no shelter. Rained nearly all night. Were ordered into line this morning at 5 and remained until day light. There seems to be a battle pending in this vicinity. When the attack will be made I have no Idea. We have revielle at 4 o'clock in the morning in order to be ready for a attack at any moment.

Last Lord's day our brigade (14th) went out Ten miles towards Silver Springs to guard a forrage train which was well loaded with corn, and returned to camp about night without any "hair breadth scapes" or even seeing any of the "butternut tribe."[1] We have been drawing some clothing for the last few days. I have drawn one pr. pants and another blanket, so I am pretty well fixed, except [for] a rubber blanket. We have drawn a few, [but] issued them to men who had no tents.

You may want to know how I like Soldiering by this time! Very well, was not the society so awful. Gambling is the common practice of nearly all and swearing is the common dialect of the Soldier. There is but few men in our company consisting of Forty Five men who do not habitually swear. Those four are Frank Bartlet,[2] [the] two Reeds[3] and myself. Sammy Shanower,[4] one of my old favorites who formerly used no bad language is now as bad as any of his ass[o]ciates. A few evenings since while standing out doores, the moon and stars shining out brightly and every thing delightfuly pleasant in every direction, the snow white tents were lighted up. And when I knew how the inmates of those "portable dwellings" were spending that beautiful Evening I could but think of those whited Sepulchers which are so fair without but within are dead men's bones.

But I must go and draw rations and this must go out to night. My health is good, as is the boys generally. Go[o]d night. My love to all. A kiss to our little folks and one to mother. Ever your own

G.W. Squier

1. "Butternut" was a term used prior to the war to refer to people (especially those of Southern origin) who lived in southern Illinois, Indiana, and Ohio. During the war, the expression commonly was applied to Confederates, especially Rebel soldiers, whose clothing—like that of the original Butternuts—was often a light-brown color, owing to the use of dye made from butternuts or walnuts. At times, as in Letter 13 in chapter 2, it was applied to Northerners who were sympathetic to the Confederacy.
2. Pvt. Francis Bartlett of Newville, who joined the company at its organization and served out his three-year term.
3. Pvts. Joseph V. and Samuel W. Reed of Wolcottsville, both of whom joined the company at its organization and served full three-year terms.
4. Pvt. Samuel A. Shanower of Wolcottsville, who joined the company for three years at its organization and then extended his enlistment. He was mustered out September 14, 1865, as the company's first sergeant.

LETTER 16

Camp Near Nashville, Tenn. Dec. 24th, 1862

Dear Ellen,

This morning we received marching orders. With three days rations and every thing packed [we are] ready to march, but as yet we are here. I will write a few lines as it may be some time before I shal have another opportunity of writing. There are all preperations being made for a fight. The sick have all been sent to town (Nashville), cartridge boxes replenished, extra nurses detailed. I of course do not know who will be the attacking party, but sighns appear to indicate a moovement of our forses on Murfreesborrow. If that be so we shall probably have a "hard fight." Yesterdy we marched out 14 mils. and return as escort for forraging train. Saw no rebbels but were very, very tired when we finally got home.

Well I herdly know what to write. I write so often. There is nothing exciting going on and prospects generally are rather derk. Tomorrow is Christmas. One year ago we were on the border of the slave states in sight of Indiana soil. One year has passed with its variations, one year of hardships, privations, and fatigues, and the prospects of peace is not as fair to day as then. There is now no room to doubt that the President's proclimation of emancipation, though in itself right and intende[d] for good, has come fer short of his and many others' wishes and expections. That proclimation will without the shadow of a doubt add one hundred thousand men to the rebbels' army and take nearly as many *from* our army.[1] Men are deserting every night by scores, mostly from the Ky. regiment. There is now about 40,000 Kentucky troops in the field. On the first of Feb. there will not be 10,000 found willing to peril their lives to, as they say, free the "Nigger," and many, very many from the free states are very little better. Many in our regt. and in Company D say that if the Proclimation be put in force they will no longer carry a musket. And I know that there is a strong opposing party north. The[se] facts togethe[r] with our late reverses [in] Virginia cast a gloom over our whole army.[2]

But I must adjourn for the pres[en]t. It is evening and I must finish this for we shal probably leave tomorrow as there is strong indications of an attack tomorrow. Tattoo is now beatin[g] and I must close. I received your letter No. 5 yesterday and was *so* glad that your heal[th] is getting so much better. It seems rather st[ran]g[e] to hear you tell of washing without making you sick, as it may seem strange to hear *me* tell of marching 20 mils. a day. Write often. A day or two sinc[e] I sent a picture to W.[3] Has [he] received it? Good night dear one and may Heaven bless and protect you is the prayer of your affectionate

George

O! Yes, there is several of the boys enlisting in the regular Corps, Nathan Rex among the number.[4]

1. In September 1862, President Lincoln issued the preliminary Emancipation Proclamation, announcing that unless the Confederates abandoned their attempt to leave the Union by January 1, 1863, he would declare free all slaves then being held in the Confederacy. Lincoln based his action on the president's power as commander in chief to employ emancipation to help suppress a rebellion. For that reason, the proclamation could not be applied to areas loyal to the Federal government. Antislavery extremists, ignoring the fact that slavery in the United States was protected by the Constitution, criticized the president for not doing enough to end the South's "peculiar institution."

   Many Federal soldiers—especially men from the loyal slave states (including Kentucky) and the Midwest—had enlisted to save the Union, not to overturn slavery. They resented having the war expanded to become a war of black liberation. There was some discontent in the army, although not on the scale Squier believed. See the comments from Lt. Hiram King of Company H of the 44th Indiana in Willey, *Iron 44th*, 87–88.

2. In July 1865, after the conclusion of the war, several men of the 44th Indiana went to prison rather than serve on the same guard detail with black troops. "The Hoosiers . . . who had fought for nearly four years, and helped to gain freedom for the slave[,] were willing the darkies should have their liberty, but did not, and still do not, want negroes brought up to an equal with the whites," wrote one veteran of the regiment. See Willey, *Iron 44th*, 121–23, 125.

   The "late reverses [in] Virginia" refers to the Battle of Fredericksburg on December 13, in which the Federals were defeated with a loss of more than twelve thousand men.

3. "W." is unidentified except for the context; Squier may have been referring to his son Wilber.

4. The "regular Corps" refers to the permanent, professional "Regular Army." The 44th Indiana and most of the Union troops were, by contrast, part of the "volunteer force" raised for service only in the Civil War. Pvt. Nathan Rex of Hall's Corners, transferred from the 44th Indiana to the 15th United States Infantry Regiment on December 24, 1862.

Chapter 2. 1863

ↆ

LETTER 1

Battle field Near Murfreesborrow Jan. 4th, 1862 [1863]

Dear Ellen,

Through an all merciful providence I am still alive after eight days hard fighting.[1] Murfreesborrow has fallen. Our loss is as yet unknow[n]. The 44th has lost in killed, wounded and missing is 142. We took into the field 281.[2] Shell, Perkins, Foote,[3] and Collier[4] are all right. I [will] borrow an envelop. [I] take this scrip of paper from my pocket, well knowing how anxious you will feell. I will write as soon as possible.

George

Gen. Rosecrans is to day the Greatest man in our Government. Long may he live. He never mooves on the Lord's day. John Casebeer is well.

George

1. The Battle of Murfreesboro, or Stones River, took place December 31, 1862–January 2, 1863. As indicated in Letter 2 below, Squier is counting the maneuvers immediately prior to the battle to get his "eight days."
2. According to Lt. Col. Simeon C. Aldrich, who commanded the regiment in the battle, the unit's strength was 316. He first (January 5, 1863) reported the unit's loss as 10 killed, 56 wounded, and 47 missing. Later some of the missing turned up and the casualties were reduced to 10 killed, 56 wounded, and 25 missing. *OR*, vol. 20, pt. 1, 203, 601.
3. Probably Pvt. Abraham Z. Foot from Harlan, who served out a full three-year enlistment.
4. Either Pvt. John W. Collier from Hall's Corners or Pvt. James Collier of Kendallville. The former reenlisted and served until September 14, 1865. The latter was promoted to second lieutenant in January 1863 and to first lieutenant in June 1863. He was dismissed on August 13, 1863.

Maj. Gen. William S. Rosecrans, commander of the Army of the Cumberland from October 1862 to October 1863. Courtesy of the Lincoln Museum, Fort Wayne, Indiana.

LETTER 2

Camp Near Murfreesborrow, Tenn. Jan. 5th, 1863

Dearest Ellen,

   On the 26th day of December, 1862, at 8 A.M., the call beat to strike tents, load baggage <a>nd be ready to march. Rain from 9 until 11 and <at> 1 A.M. [P.M.] we took up our line of march, "en rout" <for> Murfreesboro. How many, how very ma[n]y who started on that day full of life, joyous and happy, now sleeps beneath the soil in a stra[nge] land, with nothing to mark their resting place save a little mound of Earth which a few month's time will wholy obliterate? We marched 7 mils. in sight of Laverne, wher [we] camp without tents, oil cloths or blankets (as we took nothing but the indispensables). Rain nearly all night. Consequently there was little sleep for the many thousand who were about to offer up their lives for their cou[ntr]y.

Good Saturday morning at length came, when there might have been seen crawling from their holes creatures that put one in mind of so many drowned rats. But it soon stops raining and soon do the boys recover their wonted spirits. In front and to our right we hear the continual booming of cannon and the crackling of musketry, which warn us that the work has allready comen[ced]. At noon we are ordered into line. Marched out to the road. Stacked armes, awaiting orders to mo[ve] on. In half an hour the rain is comeing in <?> and those who have no overcoats are soon <wet?> to the skin. But fortunately for me I have an ex<tra> one which will stand six hours of heavy rai<n>.

About 3 P.M. we moove on and now begin[s] the unmistakable evidences that our further <advance?> had been disputed. Trees torn asunder, houses de<stroyed>, dead horses, and little mounds of Earth that mark the spot where some brave fellow sleeps the "sleep that knows no waking." How often have I been reminded of the lines "Soldier rest thy warfare o'er," &c.[1] We moove on in [evening?] on the Murfreesbor[o] pike, where we bear to the left. March about 4 miles. Camp about 7 o'clock near a large fi<eld> in a very pretty wood lot. Get our supper ma<de>. Down our bed, which is rather primitiv<e>, only requireing a rail or a smoothe stone for a pill<ow>. And was just "retireing to our virtuous couches" when the order came for Cos. D & B to go on o<ut> post duty. After due amount of grumbling at <the> amount of duty to be done, we get into line, ma<rch> about 1 ½ mils. and make our "couch" on a rich old planter's premises. After stationing our outposts, the reserve built up [a] good comfortable fire of the cedar <ra>ils of which there is abundence. The night was cold, <our> clothes wet, but in spite of this most of the boys <s>oon were lost to all trouble in the kind embr[ace] of sleep. But I cannot slepp cold so I kept up <f>ires for others less sensitive to discomforts. About <?> o'clock I heard a solitary cock, moore wakeful <tha>n his brothers, give one loud, long, but unfortunate <crow?>. Now there was little sleep for any of the boys. From that time until day light all hands were busily engaged [in] catching, picking, roasting without salt, and eating. And when the sun was up scarcely a living thing was left to greet the eyes of anxious secesh but what was to be seen wearing the "blue coats." Chickens, ducks, & turkeys, with an occasional fine mutton, all nicely dressed, hung suspended from all most every tree, while beneath them was feathers to the right of us, feathers to the left of us, feathers in front of us, feathers in rear of <u>s.[2]

[It is] Sunday, pleasant, and we know it will <be> a day of rest. Ought we not to be very thankful <tha>t we are under a commander who recognizes <th>e claim of our Father to one-seventh of our time, even in the army? But Rosecrans is such a m[an].

This morning one of our best Soldiers passed away after an illness of 9 hours.[3] The day passes of[f] pleasan<tly>—nothing exciting. Pickets exchange occasional shots, nothing moore. Relieved from picket about 4 P.M., in time for dress perade, where it was announced we were now in the 2nd Brigade, 3rd division, Criten<den's> Corps, Army of the Cumberland.[4]

Monday—our regt. on <picket?>. Heavy cannonading in front and to the right. At 12 received orders to march. Cross over to the Murfrees<boro> road, and camp within Three miles from town, wit<h> few rails within a mile. And what was worse very [bad?] and here we are allmost in sight of the enemy. It is a beautiful sight to see—thousands of camp<fires?> extending in every direction as far as the eye <can> reach. It is feed time, and having drank a cup of coffee, eaten some crackers (not butter crackers), and so will turn in.

Tuesday comes and with it rain, which every time [is] disagreeable, but it does not prevent the work of death. At an early hour cannonading is hea<rd> on our extreme right, which soon extends along the whole length of the line. But there was little done except artillery fireing through [the] day. Gen. Rosencrans superintends the work. The day passes without advantage to either party, except we had succeeded in throwing thre[e] temporary bridges across Stone river, which will enable <us> to cross that streem and attack the enemy on his <side?>.

Wednesday, Dec. 31st, long to be remembered, comes. The su<n> rises, clear after several days of funeral gloom, ruptur<ing> mists which hung like silver curtains over the hills and glistening along the serried line of [bayonets?], which glittered in the morning light like countless jewel[s], bathing the gay banners which floated along the line with a flood of refulgence and lighting up the emeral<d> fringes of the beatiful cedars which enclose the field. <As> far as the eye can reach stand the two vast armies, silent and motionless. Standing on an eminence w<here> I could see all this splen-did array it allmost seem<ed> that instead of foes drawn up for battle, to be s<ome> grand pageantry of display, some holiday perrade. <I> forget—I had intended to confine myself to the action of our own Regt., well knowing that this, the greatest fight of the West, will be portrayed by many abler pens than mine, and that I should make a miserable display of the grand scenery, noble [?] of blood and misery and death. But then perhaps it may be interesting to you, so I may go somewhat into details but confine myself to what passed under my observation.

At 7 o'clock we fell in, march<ed> to our left nearly ¼ mile, [and were] ordered to halt. While stand<ing> we hear a small volley of musketry directly in our <re>ar. In another inst. another and another, sharper and heavier. All is a<n>xiety. Soon the rattle of musketry is deadened by the roar of artillery. Many anxious faces were there in those ranks then, for it was feered we were attacked in force in our rear. Soon Gen. C.'s <aide?> came galloping up. Then the order "file left, d<ouble q>uick march," and away our Brigade started. An<d we w>ent run[ning] in the direction of the fireing. One <ran> through cedar bushes, up hill and down, <ove>r rocks, through mud and water, and finally arriv<ed> at the scene of disturbence when we found all [?] the cause. Wheeler's Cavalry [had] made a dash on <our> train, capturing some 60 or 70 waggons, which were <all> retaken.[5] We rest a few minutes, countermarch, and form line of battle near the center of our lines. By this time—9—it was one incessant thun-der of artil[lery]. After a few minutes rest skirmishers are sent out, and our line mooves slowly to the front through allmost impenitrable thi[ck]ets of cedar briars, weeds, &c&c. Now we emerge into a large open field covered with high weeds. Here t<he> skirmishing commences. Steadily we ad<van>ce across that field which was soon to drink <t>he blood of so many breve men.[6]

Now I will en[dea]vor to give you an Idea of our position. We are in a la[r]ge open field. Dir[e]ctly to our righ[t] & left the clearing extends for half a mile. In advance and to the right is a neck of woods running up into the field some 30 rods. Our line on the right when we advance will lack 20 rods of resting on that woods. Some 80 rods directly in front is the termination <of th>e field, and beyond is heavy timber. The skirmish<ing> now is decidedly brisk, bullets frequent<ly> whistleing over [our] heeds. We moove up to the fence, ordered to lay [down] the skirmishers' advance in order to feel the po<sit>ion of the enemy. In 10 minutes ordered to rise and ad<va>nce. Down goes the fence and we s<low>ly climb over the fence and whiz chuck went a ball and one of Co. D fell dead <and another?> wounded. [We] are in the w<eeds?>, through among the trees perhaps 100 rods. The e<ne>my is distinctly seen. When within 80 rods of their lines we are ordered down, then to raise and fire. We had fired but three rounds when a great blunder was discovered. We were flanked on our right and in five minutes we would have been prisoners. The order was given to retreat. There is no set of men who can endur<e> a flank fire. The 44th, for the first time pa<nic-> stricken, became perfectly unmanageable. Away they run, <the> officers vainly endeavoring to rally at the fence where lay the 13th O[hio] as our reserve. Col. Williams sees that he no longer commands the 44th and in his agony he cries "O! Heavens! Can it be?"[7] So I was left behind, using all my endeavors to stop the men of our Co. but to no effect. I rushed in front of the line, drew the bayonet, and commanded them to halt. They paused slightly. Said I, "can you desert those collors," pointing to our flag some distance in the rear. Two men stoped and w<ith> myself returned. <We> took our position with the <soldiers?> who still stood firm by our old tattered, <and> torn but not the less dear old flag. The <rest?> of the boys I did not see for hours.

No<w t>he enemy opens his fire in earnest. Volley after volley they pour down upon us—from the fro<n>t and right a perfect storm of bullets, more than mortal man could endure. The gallant 13th broke, <a>nd when I looked round for our collors, no flag was to be seen. Then comenced a perfect stampede—men running for dear life, disengaging haversacks, cartridge boxes, canteens, overcoats, guns, everything that could impede their progress. On, on they or rather we rush while the enemy fires in a shower of grape and <c>annister. I retrated directly back for a short dis<tance>, then filed to the right, and was soon ou<t of> range of the enemy's <fi>re, when I stoped to rest. Looking over the fi[e]ld, you might see men running with all their might sudenly disappeer among the weeds, having been ov<er>taken by the death dealing grape and canister.

In <ma>king my way back to the rear I fell in with Ezra W<or>den.[8] As we pass along there may be seen hundreds of poore fellows awfully mutillated—shot in every conceiveable way—one from our own co. less one finger, another with his left hand carried away by a canister shot, another the ball passes in at the mouth, tearing the lips frightfully, performing rather severe dental opperations and passes out just in front of the left ear.

When first I saw our lines giving away, I felt sick, desperate, thinking that perhaps the day was lost. But as I fall back <an>d see line after line stretched as far as the eye could rea<ch>, all laying close to the ground to prevent the enemy seeing <their> position, and heavy <artillery?> drawn up under cover of the hill ready at the p<roper m>oment to run up to the summit and do its <?> duty. Now I am standing on the hill and what a scene <is there> before me. A short distance in front are still to be <seen a> few of those vanquished troops who a short time a<go w>ere so confident of victory, now making very good time <pursuing?> safety, some allmost naked, having thrown [away] hats, coats, <and> everything but pants and shirt. Some are wounded, others <are> not. Further out comes thousands of the enemy, shooting down the flying men, whooping, bellowing, and running, though in good o<rd>er. On, on they come, little dreeming of the fate awaiting <the>m. Now turning my eye to the left, I see Capt. Lommis (com<ma>nder-in-chief of all the artillery)[9] looking calmly down on the scene, now again looking upward. The enemy is mooving slow<ly>, and as he thinks, surely across the field. On they come, l<ine> after line, to [?]. Looking around, Capt. Loomis is just waiting to give orders. The artillery mooves rapidly up to the brow of the hill. [?] thought they were now unlimbered [and] wheeled into position. Down goes the charge of canister and the men await anxiously the order to fire. On comes the enemy. Nothing opposes his progres[s] until within about 400 yards, when the pieces of artillery thundered forth and away went the Iron balls rolling through the ranks of the enemy, mowing them down by hundreds. They falter, but their ranks were immediately closed, and another and another and another volley belches forth from those Iron monsters. It is more than even the stubborn rebbels can not long withstand. Again they falter. They fix bayonets, and then I knew there was to be Bloody work. The order is g<iv>en to charge on the battery which was poring its galling fire upon them. On they rush, with yells which was heerd above the din of battl. Confident that soon they would be able to man the death dealing instruments, [they met with?] disappointment when within 80 yds. <of the> battery, what was their suprise at seeing a line of men raise as out <of the> earth with bristling bayonets. In an instant the guns are leveled, and away went a shower of lead which nearly annihilate[d] it. [This] was <m>ore than mortal man could withstand. [On?] they go, our men after them [?] at an awful rate the tide is turned. The victory at this point at least is ours. I now turn in search of the regt. Finally find [it] or what is left of it— [?] consisted of 6 men and one officer. It is now nearly night and am I sorry<. . . .> that I cam out all right. My health is not very good, perhaps owing to exposure and some fatigue. I will at my earliest convenience—I will endeavor to furnish you with the second *"volume."*[10] This has been written at odd times and I had no memorandum to note down perticular[s] so I had to depend entirely upon my memory, which you know is rather poor dependance. I will here say that I was in all the fights in which our regt. was engaged and *moore*.

I received yours of the 24th ult. yesterdy and was delighted to find you getting along so well. Give my love to all, especially to Mothers (I mean both of them). Yesterdy I sent to Nashville a very fine oil painting to be expressed to Fort Wayne to you. I intended it for [?] as she allways takes such good care of her things. When once un-

rolled do not roll it up aga[in], as the paint will crack—warm it well before unroll-
ing. Write often and remember ever your affectionate and loving

George

Don't let other folks see this awful scrawl.

1. These quotations derive from Walter Scott, *The Lady of the Lake: A Poem,* 2d ed. (Edinburgh, 1810), 38.
2. A play on Alfred, Lord Tennyson's "Charge of the Light Brigade": "Cannon to the right of them; Cannon to the left of them . . . . "
3. A search of the roster did not reveal any man in the regiment who died on December 28, 1862, although there were several who died during the war and whose date of death is not recorded in the roster. It is possible—although unlikely—that Squier referred to someone outside the regiment.
4. The other regiments assigned to the brigade were the 86th Indiana and the 13th and 59th Ohio. See *OR,* vol. 20, pt. 1, 174–82 for the army's organization in late December 1862.
5. Confederate cavalry under Brig. Gen. (later Maj. Gen.) Joseph Wheeler attacked a Fed-eral wagon train on the Nashville–Murfreesboro road near Overall's Creek. Wheeler re-ported that the fighting went on in the area for the rest of the day. *OR,* vol. 20, pt. 1, 449, 959, 967–68, 970. Marion Butler of Company A (*Story,* 265), recorded that the regiment's fight with the cavalry lasted only about ten minutes and that the Hoosiers then returned to the main battle. Rebel horsemen probably made other efforts to get at the wagons, hence Wheeler's statement. See Letter 8.
6. The main body of the Confederate army had attacked the right of the Federal line. Crit-tenden's troops, who had been on the left of the position, rushed to the right to meet the Rebel assault. Although bent back at almost a right angle, the Northern line held after some very hard fighting. See Peter Cozzens, *No Better Place to Die: The Battle of Stones River* (Urbana, 1990). The report covering the 44th Indiana is in *OR,* vol. 20, pt. 1, 601–2.
7. Col. William C. Williams, who had succeeded Reed as regimental commander on No-vember 27, 1862, was captured on January 2, 1863. After being exchanged, he resigned, effective May 12, 1863.
8. Pvt. Ezra Worden of Hall's Corners, who served with the company until discharged March 3, 1864. See Letter 5.
9. Capt. Cyrus Loomis, commanding the artillery of the 3d Division of Crittenden's com-mand, not of the entire army. He was later promoted to colonel with date of rank Octo-ber 8, 1862. On June 25, 1865, he was made a brevet brigadier general for war service.
10. See Letter 3.

LETTER 3

Camp near Murfreesboro, Tenn. Jan. 11th, 1863

Dearest Ellen,

    I had allmost thought to wait until I heard from you whether you succeeded in getting "through" with the doubtless "in a most" interminable scrawl of the first

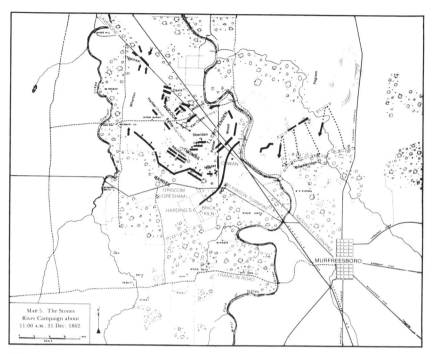

The Stones River Campaign, about 11 A.M., December 31, 1862. From Stones River: Bloody Winter in Tennessee *by James Lee McDonough. Used with permission.*

volume of the battle near Murfreesboro, and [if?] the second *vol.* would be acceptable. But having leasure I will venture to proceed. I think I left you just as I started in search of the regt. Well, in due process of time I found the remnant of the 44th. It is now about 4 P.M. and we are moving off to the right, where but a short time sin[c]e men were engaged in deadly conflict, and of which the[re] is still abundent signs— muskets, rifles, cartridge boxes, caps, &c&c., with not a few of the dead and wounded of the enemy. Just in front of Co. D is one of those brave but misguided creatures who was pressed through the breast with a rifle ball, his pale face upturned to heaven, the glassy eyes still open and his left hand raised, lips open as if about to speak. Just in our rear is another, shot through the head and still breathing. Both of these had their pockets turned inside out and every thing of value taken, which is no uncommon circumstance. It is a cold night and we are doomed to spend the night without fire, with no coffee for supper, nothing but hard bread and raw "sow belly." At 11 we are called into line. [We] march one mile to the rear, where we [are] allowed fire. At 2 we draw rations of coffee, sugar and flour. The ballance of the night is spent in baking (on a board), roasting and eating, [nodding?] &c.

Thursday, Jan. 1st is finally come—cold, clear, and pleasant. At sunrise we are called

into line. [We] march of[f] to the left across Stone River and after considerable skirmishing across a large open field take our position in a small strip of woods of some
twenty rods in width. In front of this is a large [corn?] field. To our right on a slight
rise of ground is planted the 3rd Wisconsin battery of 6 Parrot guns (the best gun in
the service).[1] The day passes of[f] with little excitement. Sharp skirmishing continues through the [day] but with little effect on either side. When the enemy would
get rather saucy, our little *pieces* would drop a few shell in their midst, or perhaps
send a charge of grape rattling over across the field, which invariably had a salutary
effect. At night our pickets [were] doubled to prevent surprise. As darkness comes
on, the firing gradually dies away and then finally seaces entirely. Cedar rails are close
at hand and plenty, and soon bright fires spring up [the] whole length of our line (I
mean our brigade line), the right of which rested on Stone River and extending
through the woods [as] I before mentioned, and the left extended nearly to a public
road running from the ford to the Lebanon pike. For some cause I could not get
sleeppy (though I did not sleep 5 mints. the night before) until near midnight. Then
I went to the rear in the solitude of the night to thank that kind Father for his goodness and for my future aid and protection. What a comfort it is to have so kind a
friend to whom we can unbosem all troubles, one who will feel for, sy[m]pathi[ze]
with, and comfort us. It [is] dark and for the present I must close.

Now to proceed—at midnight there was a sole report of a musket on our extreme
right. Another and another quickly follow, and soon our whole picket line is one blaze
of musketry. The main force was soon in line and all expected a night attack. The
fireing continues a short time, then dies away, and in fifteen minutes after the discharge of the first gun all was silent as before.

Friday morning, Jan. 2 comes beautiful and bright. How many, how v[ery] many
saw on that morning for the last time that glori[ous] orb arise, giving life and beauty
to all the earth, [un]til that brighter sun shal arise, until the m[orni]ng of the resu-
rection shal come, when the nati[ons] of the dead shal awake, beyond which there
will be no [m]ore wars, no severing of tender ties, no parting[s] such [as] allmost tear
the life from out the human heart.

As the mist clears away and the two armies can see each other, the fireing again commences. [It] continues until about 11 A.M., when it gradually dies away. But we can
distinctly see the enemy mooving in various directions, evidently preparing for an
attack. About 12, "boom" went a gun, and a shell came whistleing by and burst far in
our rear. Another and another and still they come. He is feeling for our position, endeavoring to provoke an answer from our guns, but without effect. In fa[c]t, the artillery that had occupied position in our line had fallen back to the bank of the river.[2]

At 2:45 o'clock the skirmishing again commences with redoubled fury. At half past
two it is quiet, and the boys generaly think there will be no hard fighting this P.M.,
and I with many others take off my haversack to take something for the inner man.
At 3 P.M. our skirmishers are attack[ed] in force. The men are ordered into line, flat
on their fa[ce]s. In position to the right can be seen the enemy, mooving up steadily

and in excellent order at a right shoulder shift-armes. On they come, line after line
to the number of 8, making their ranks sixteen men deep. Their line rested on Stone
River but did not extend far enough to our left to come in contact with our regt.
Consequently, I had a very good opportunity of witnessing the awful conflict going
on to our right (as I was not obliged to lay down). The enemy mooves up, their flags
waving defiantly, confident of an easy victory. When within about 100 yds. of our
line, our men rais from the ground, wave the stars and stripes, an[d] pour in a most
effective fire, judged from the number of men who disappeared among the weeds
and cornstalks. Their first line (what is left of it) fires into our ranks and disappear[s]
in the weeds. The second line marches forward over the prostrate front line—fire[s]
and lay[s] down. The third line marches up and so on through, which made one
continuous shower of bullets. Add to this grape and canister from twelve guns and
you may perhaps conceive the heat of the possition occupied by the 35 & 17th Ind.,
the 57th[?] & 64th regts., while we were in comperative safty.[3] So[o]n the order came
for our regt. to fire right oblique, when we open on them with what effect I do not
know. I was exhorting the boys to fire low, keep cool, &c., and did not hear the order [to] retreat. And when by chance I looked around, I found [t]hat Co. D. was
alone. Lieut. Shell having disappeared, said "b[oys], fire your loads out and run."
Turning round, our [line] was just disappearing over a hill. [I] told the men to follow [the] collors, and away we went pell mell over the field. [At the] time, though I
run, I was not scared. All over [the] field was one dence mass of confusion. Men
running [with all] their might. A little to my left I saw a man [leap?] in the air and
fall heavily to the ground, dead. Still [another man] claps his hand upon his breast,
turns quickly half the way round and falls, to rise no more. In front I see a fellow fall
flat on his face, and as I pass see that he is [hor]ribly wounded by gun shot in the
bowels. Another drops his gun, claps his [rig]ht hand to his left arm, and redoubles
his speed. Another which lay in my way had his left foot shot away. One to my left
fell with the loss of his head, the effect of a shot from one of our own guns.

By this time I had lost all traces of Co. D or any member of the 44th. On I go yes
and run to[o], bearing of[f] sharply to the right, and was soon out of range of the
enemy's fire, except [for] an occasional grape which came rattling by. Finally I gained
a high bluff on the right bank of Stone River. Looking back may be seen thousands
upon thousands of the enemy, sweeping over that open field, their banners proudly
waving (wrote and sent it in the P.M. 9 A.M., 13th—I feell awful bad this morning,
but will endeavor to finish this), their shots mingling with the din of battle. A Wis-
conson regt. is marching up to engage the enemy and I fall in to lend a helping hand
to retrieve our reverses. The enemy mooves up until near the river when two divisions (Negly's and Wood's) rais from the ground, pour one mighty volley of musketry, and rush on with charge bayonets.[4] The first line breaks [and] rushes back
through the next line, which throws it into disorder, and soon the whole army is one
dence mass of confusion. I can't write now, there is no use trying. I can only say that
we pursued them until "darkness put an end to the conflict." This ends my fighting

in the "great" battle of Stone River. At some future time perhaps I may refer to the scenes on the battle field after the fight.[5] I went all over our field the night of the battle, it being a fine moonlight night.

Now we are in camp about ½ mile north of Murfreesboro, with plenty of poor water and a scarcity of cedar rails. I believe I told you that since the fight my health has not been very good, as is the case with a great many others. Henry Kessler and his boy is among the missing.[6] Cyrene and Charly Higgins[7] are sick at Nashville. I did not throw away those things, or at least none of value—only a lot of papers sent to Tommie[8] and some maple sugar for the same, which I did neither throw away nor carry through. I "got along" very well. Am now very well provided for here—two wollen blankets, very good pants, a good coat, the old blouse which you have seen, an overcoat, and this morning [I] drew what I very much needed, a rubber blanket.

Perhaps you may judge from some of my former letters why I soldier? Now it is because I *can't help it,* which I think is a very good reason. Have not as much duty to do now as before the fight, as we do very little forraging or picket duty. Common guard duty does not effect my labors. Charley Wayne has resigned. Lieut. Shell is now in command of the Co. I get along with him very well since I told him that I knew my duty and was willing to do it.

Am glad to hear you have a flannel dress, as it is something you surely needed. *Perhaps* I would not like to be with you to help eat beef soup & mince pies, and perhaps I would. Am glad you have no more stock to attend to. Hope the lard and [?] may prove a [real?] cure for body gnats. If so pleas inform me, for such a discovery would be of immens value here in the army. When we came to this camp something of the kind might have been used to very good advantage by your *humble servant.* Well, I don't know as there is any thing moore to [write] at present. The w[e]ather is delightful and I wish I felt well to enjoy it. Give my love to all. A kiss to the little ones and if you wish one to your own dear self, and remember me as your loving

George

1. The 3d Wisconsin Artillery Battery was assigned to the artillery of Van Cleve's division. *OR,* vol. 20, pt. 1, 582–83.
2. After a relatively quiet New Year's Day, the Confederates made a furious attack on the Union left on January 2. As Squier relates, it was repulsed, but for part of the day it seemed that it would overrun that part of the Federal line.
3. Squier confuses the regiments to his right. The troops were the men of the 3d Brigade of his division. From left to right, the regiments were the 79th Indiana, the 35th Indiana, the 8th Kentucky, and the 51st Ohio. The brigade was commanded by Col. Samuel W. Price. See the map in Cozzens, *No Better Place,* 184.
4. Maj. Gen. James S. Negley and Maj. Gen. Thomas J. Wood. Negley's division had been ordered to the left to support Van Cleve. Negley's report is in *OR,* vol. 20, pt. 1, 408.

Wood's division was part of Crittenden's command. Wood's report is in *OR,* vol. 20, pt. 1, 461–62.

5. See Letters 4, 6, and 8 (as continued).

6. See chapter 1, Letter 14, note 2.

7. Charles H. Higgins of Hall's Corners, who reenlisted and served until September 14, 1865.

8. Unidentified other than by context.

LETTER 4

Camp Near Murfreesboro, Tenn. Jan. 24th, 1863

Dear Ellen,

I have nothing to do and of course can't do any thing else than write, for it seems the only way of killing time—though I allmost fear you will think our correspondence rather expen[sive] (as *you* have to pay postage both ways). If that be the case, just mention it and I will endeavor to "hold up". It seems an age since the arrival of your last letter (No. 6). I ought long since to have learned the important lesson to "wait." I think I shal by the expiration of that "Three years or during the war[. . . .]"[1]

I think I left of[f] at the close of the fight of Fridy, Jan. 2nd. I did think I would give you a few "items" of the field after the fight. And then perhaps it would be anything but agreeable to you for me to particularize, so I will not. The fighting ceased at dark. The moon shone out clear and pleasant, giving death doubly a ghostly and "deathly" appearance. Strolling along over the field, which lay thickly strewn with the gallant dead, my attention was often drawn to the wounded, who beg[g]ed to be remooved or at least to throw a blanket over them as they were "freezing." In a narrow strip of woods which skirted the river where there was a fire burning, some Thirty of these poor wretches had dragged themselves and lay as close as they could be packed. Not far from this place and by a large tree lay four dead "rebs." By the side of one lay a very fine British rifle. It being of the same calibre of our guns, I left my musket and took the rifle—simply exchanged with the gentleman. You know, in fifteen minutes after the fight, every rebbel's pocket was turned in and out. I relieved one of a very good pocket ink stand, which now furnishes me with ink—allso a pair of buckskin gloves, which I needed. O yes, right her[e] I will tell *you* (of cours it is a p[r]ofund secret) that on the wednesday [?] my haversack, which contained three days rations and my gloves, was rather "cumbrous," and consequently was left on the field. Lieut. Shell did not bring his off, but claims that the strap was shot off. I told the boys that I threw mine away, as I did not then feell that I should want anything more to eat—dinner is ready and so am I.

Dinner over and I feell "bett[er]," for we had warm bread and hot tea and nice ham. A real feast was it not! But to proceed. About 8 o'clock that evening I found a part of the regt. with but one man of Co. D—John Caseber. They were a little to the left of the field, near some old buildings which were used as hospitals. After taking a cup of hot coffee and eating a cracker, John and I turned in under an old shed and for the first time since we left camp slept. Rain through the night. Saturday morn[in]g waked much refreshed. On a porch in rear of the large dwelling used as hospital lay a long row of bodies of men who had died through the night from their wounds—Horrible specticle! "And what is war [but] a dark and desperate game where lives and li[m]bs and hearts and souls of men are staked for knaves."

Thus ended our active part in the Battle of Stones river. I need not speak of the conduct of our gene[r]als, as the papers will, or rather is doing them justice but nothing moore. I really believe that should Gen. Rosecran<s> tell the men they could wade the Atlant[ic] Ocean without wetting their feet, it would be believed. For instance, he ordered that there be no moore rails burned, as we might need them for breastworks. "All right, Old Rose's head is right, he knows what he's about." Had Buel issued that order it would hardly been as much heeded as the South wind blowing.

"All qu[i]et along the Potomac to night"[2]—no excitement, every thing miserably peaceful. Rumer says that Bragg is reinforced by 45,000 men from Fredricksburgh, and 20,000 from Vicksburgh.[3] Also that Gen. Grant's fleet lays at Smithland at the mouth of the Cumberland river,[4] and that Burnside is again marching on to Richmond.[5] Allso "that there is great things soon to be announced to the world." Cyrene is still at Nashville. Bert is quite well. The Wordens we know nothing of, but it is the general opinion that they gave themselves up—Ezra and Ira I mean—Sanford was not in the fight.[6] The Kesslers we know nothing of moore than Martin fell out early in the Morning long before we were hot into action. Henry was seen after our retreat (or rather run) far in the rear and out of danger. Charles Higgins is in the convalesent Hospital at Nashville. They say that Geo. Maxwell[7] is paying his "distresses" to Sister Lomira. I believe it of cours over the left. Don't think I should much like him for a brother. I received a letter from Myron[8] a few days since but have not answered it. I must clos[e], so good by. Write often. Love to all, and partic[ularly] your own dear self.

G.W. Squier

1. Northern soldiers usually enlisted for "three years or the war." In 1864, most of those who had originally entered service for three years "veteranized" to serve for the rest of the war.
2. "All Quiet along the Potomac Tonight" was a popular Civil War song.
3. Gen. Braxton Bragg commanded the main Confederate army in the West 1862–63. The rumor of his receiving reinforcements was false. In fact, troops had been sent away from his army to reinforce the Confederates in Mississippi.
4. At the time, Grant was based in Memphis, Tennessee. His attention was focused on capturing Vicksburg, Mississippi, and reestablishing national control all along the Mississippi River.
5. Maj. Gen. Ambrose E. Burnside commanded the North's main army in Virginia. On January 20, he began an effort to maneuver around the Confederate army in his front. By January 28, heavy rains had forced him to abandon his efforts.

6. See Letter 2, note 8. Pvt. Ira A. Worden was captured, paroled, exchanged, captured again, and died in the prisoner-of-war camp at Andersonville, Georgia, on June 25, 1864. Cpl. Sanford Worden, also from Hall's Corners, served until May 27, 1865. See Letter 5.
7. Geo. Maxwell is unidentified except by context.
8. Myron is unidentified except by context.

LETTER 5

Camp near Murfreesboro, Tenn. Feb. 3rd, 1863

Dear Ellen,

Yours of 25th ult. came to hand last night. I have written to Mrs. Kessler. Her husband is at Anapolis, Md. being paroled, as also is Martin and the three Wordens—Confidential—you wish to know how I came to command the Co. If I conveyed that idea during Wednesday's fight, it was through some blunder. My place in ranks on the march is the right of the company, acting as right guide. In battle my place is in rear of the Co. as file closer—to assist in giving orders, to keep the ranks well dressed, &c. I am not allowed to fire. And of course in case of rallying after the ranks are broken it is part of my duty to assist in restoring order. Perhaps it was something I said about my endeavors to stop the Co. that led you to suppose I commanded on that day. Is that the case! From the time the regt. reformed after the flight until Fridy about noon I commanded the Co., as Shell was among the missing. On Thursday we heard from him about *three miles to the rear*. He was then making a straight line for Nashville, but was doubtless stoped by the guards. At least, that is the generel opinion among the boys. About our position being on the righ[t] instead of the left—in my letter did [I] not mention being ordered back to retake our train which had been captured by Wheeler's cavalry? By the time we had marched back to the right of our lines, McCook's[1] right had been turned and our division was ordered up in its place, or rather to the right of his remaining Corps.

It is generally beli[e]ved that Martin Kessler and the three Wordens gave themselves up. Martin K. & Sanford W. was not in the fight. They fell out early in the morning, and yet they were captured on Fridy. When ordered to retreat, Ezra and Ira instead of obeying the order took shelter behind a tree in *front* of our lines. On Wednesday one of our Co. asked Ezra if he was not going back to the Co. He said, "let the young men who have no families fight." Very affectionate, that Ezra—is not as well liked in the Co. as either of his brothers. But I think I have written quite enough "scandle" for one time. You may wish to know how I felt during the fight. Once on Wednesdy I was very badly scared—that was the only time.

The weather here now is cold. Last night was the coldest night of the season—froze hard enough for the mud to bear up a man. Dinner is allmost ready. The mail will soon go out, so I must close. Write often. I don't know [how] ma[n]y blunders I might have made in my description of the battl, as I did not look it over. The reason I did not mention Albert Jackson in my first line of [the] 4th was he was not in the fight. He is doing Provost guard duty. Good by. My love to all.

G.W. Squier

1. Maj. Gen. Alexander McDowell McCook commanded the right of the Union line at Stones River. It was his position that the Confederates attacked on December 31, and it was to his assistance that the 44th Indiana and other troops were sent that day.

LETTER 6

Camp Near Murfreesboro, Tenn. Feb. 5th, 1863

Dear Ellen,

Yours of 26th ult. (No. 11) came duly to hand (last night), and of course I must write to day and will endeavor to answer your questions, or so far at least as I am able. You have doubtless read the or[i]ginal plan of Gen. Rosencran's for the fight on Wednesday. It was for Gen. McCook (who commanded the right) to make a brisk demonstration on the right to draw the enemy['s] attention to that point, and at the same time for Gen. Crienton's [Crittenden's] Corps (consisting of three divisions) to cross Stones river, form his lines, and swing around into Murfreesboro. McCook was ordered if to[o] hotly engaged to fall back slowly, so as to give C. time to swing a[round?] and get in the enemy's works. You allso I presume know that during the night the enemy had massed his for[c]es on his left and at daylight engaged McCook in tremendous force right here.[1]

I may be [?] of our lines. Our right rested on or perhaps extended across the Franklin pike (this is the road on which McCook appr[oach]ed the town), extended along to the left, first through a strip of woods, then across a small open field, then through a cedar thicket (those cedar thickets are not in the heavy timber—they ar[e] usually on some side [hill?] or rocky place), then across an old cotton field, crosing the Nashvill pike, the NC R.R. [Nashville–Chattanooga Railroad], and extending through another smal thicket across an old corn field, with the left resting on Stones river. Vancleave's division lay in the rear some 80 rods, perhaps not so far and nearly one hundred rods to the right of Stones river and on up the hill. In rear is cedar thicket. Directly in front and to the right is a large open field. Here is where I could see both lines. In front and to the left is the small thick[et] I mentioned. This was our position on Wednesday morning early. You of cours know that McCook did not hold the enemy in his position, nor did he fall back "slowly." His right fell back in great disorder, and his whole line was driven in nearly to Murfreesboro pike. The enemy followed up some distance and formed his lines in the woods in front of that open field. This was done while our division was attending to Wheeler's Cavalry, who you know had made a dash on and captured our train. As I said, we were marched up the pike to where McCook's men were re-forming. We formed on their right—that is, Van Cleave's division. By this time you will se[e] that we ar[e] nearly "whipped," and nothing but the allmost "Supreme" Generalship of [our] Comander saved the day.

But I am not answering questions very fast am I? And you are allmost "dead" with curiosity by this time, without doubt. When we marched out to fight you will doubtle[ss] see by what I have said that our lines have changed direction materially sin[c]e the fight began. Instead of running in straight lines, they are running nearly in the shape of a horseshoe.[2] When we marched out ac[r]oss the field, we were the extreme right, but the line was being continued to the right and [was] nearly parallel with the Nashville road. I think that we were sent out to engage the enemy while the new line was being completed. At any rate, when we had fallen back the lines extended far off to the right. When I spoke of filing to the right, you will remember I was retreating, and consquently my right would be towards the center of our lines. When I spoke of getting out of range of the enemy's fire, I refered to the flank fire they were pouring in with such affect. I do not know where Palmer's (Smith's old division)[3] and Wood's division of Critenden's Corps were at that time, but presume they were on the left along the river, as there was some fighting through the day at that place. We could see over the cedars from the top of *that* hill. It was perhap 75 rods from the hill to the open field, and a little farther across the field. Col. Williams, after dispairing of rallying his men, hurried to the rear. There was one Sergt. beside myself. Ezra Worden was not among the six, nor I think [were] any of your acquaintences, though I may be mistaken. A. Foote[4] was one of those who returned with me to the flag. The whole Co. fell back in the rear of the flag. The collor bearer was not shot but came off safely with the collors. Col. H.[5] of the 13th O[hio] was *not* killed while trying to rally his men, but before they had fired a shot and while they were lying by the fe[n]ce. They did not get over the fence into the woods. The Ballance of the 44th were sick, discharged, dead, deserted, on detached service, &c&c. Am very glad that you "take the papers." The ballance of your enquries I beli[e]ve I have answered in previous letters. Ask as many questions as you wish. I must close as paper is worth 50 cts. [?] and hard to get at that, and consequently I must not use moore than half a sheet at a time. I am not quite as well as usual, though quite com[for]table. Write often. In thinking over what I wrote about the fight I have thought I did not make myself out a little braver than any one else, but then I only intended it for you. I am as ever your loving

George

1. This is an accurate description of Rosecrans's plan. Each side planned to assault the right end of the enemy's line. The Confederates struck first and in great force.
2. The line of the army; not that of the regiment.
3. Maj. Gen. John M. Palmer, who commanded the 2d division of McCook's wing (or corps), and Brig. Gen. William Sooy Smith, who had commanded the same division in November and early December 1862.

4. Abraham Z. Foot of Harlan, who served out a three-year enlistment in the company.

5. Col. Joseph G. Hawkins, mortally wounded while encouraging his men December 31. See *OR*, vol. 20, pt. 1, 603. The 13th Ohio was in the brigade with the 44th Indiana.

LETTER 7

Camp Near Murfreesboro, Tenn. Feb. 7th, 1863

My own Dear Ellen,

It is [a] beautiful Spring morning after rather a cold night. The sun shines out brightly, every thing so pl[e]asent. I hardly know why I feel so *very* lonely, so depressed. Why is there such a foreboding of evil? Perhaps it is that the clouds stand heavy and still heavier over our beloved land. There is no ray of light in our political horizon. All is dark, darker than midnight, and each succeeding day but makes the darkness moore visable, but [also] reveals moore clearly the fact that we have no longer a government. Ruin, complete and utter ruin, stares us in the face. Our once proud and happy Nation is today toppling over into the abyss of Eternal distruction. The day is forever past when it was an honor to be called an American citizen. We are fast becoming a byword among the nations of the Earth. You think me excited! That I have little or no real grounds for my fears! Perhaps so—but what means that great and rapidly increasing so-called peace party of the North! What means the daily increasing discontent among the soldiers! And what means an armed mob in the state of Indiana for the avowed purpose of resisting the law![1] Think you not our enemys are aware of the divisions among the people of the Northern States! They most assuredly are. Allready are their emmissarys at work in various shapes. If you doubt it, look if you please at the course of Valindingham and Bright of our own state.[2] Who can watch their cours closely and not be forced to the conclusion that they are in [correspondence?] with the Confederate Government? And yet their principals are becoming moore popular evry day. So far have matters progressed that the confederate Congress now in session in Richmond, Va. dares to suggest to the North West the propriety of withdrawing their troops from the field and setting up a seperate Government. They offer to treat favorably with such a government—to enter into compact for mutual defence, to guarantee the f[r]ee navigation of the Mississippi River, &c&c. They [hold] up to the Pacific States & Territories the advantages of cutting loose from the old Government—that they would have the Rocky mountains to protect their Eastern lines—secureing the whole trade of the Pacific Ocean—of retaining the precious metels which are found in such abundance on the Western slope of the Rocky mountains, and allso of ridding themselves of a great and rappidly increasing public debt.[3] These are facts in the face of which who can look without fear and trembling? I have long since doubted the stability of this Government, Though there might be a republican form of Government established which would endure for ages, that would be prosperous and happy perhaps until the end of time.

I would have a republic built on the firm basis of the Bible, governed by the pure principels taught by our blessed Savior. I would not mingle *Church* and State, but I would mingle pure and undefiled religion with all the affairs of the human family. You may ask that if it is for our great national sins that this calamity is upon us. Why have the despotic Governments of Europe—who oppress the poore and favor the rich and are guilty of ma[n]y naughty acts contrary to the Scriptures—why has not God blotted them out of existence? Why has he permitted *them* to *live* and *prosper* for centurys while we, much moore Christian and far better than they (are we not rather self righteous?), scarcely exist for one generation? Look if you pl[e]ase for one moment at the difference in the form of Government. In one case a man's will is Sovereign. His word is law from which there is no appeal, and no one deres gainsay his actions. The "people" who compose [the] material pa[r]t of a nation take no part in the legislation, and consequently can in no way be held responsible for the acts of their sovereign. In the other case *every* citizen is a law maker, a legislator, and as such he is answerable before the tribunal of Heaven for his every act. Is it moore than just if he transgress the law of God! If he forgets his obligation to his Creator that he should suffer there for! And have we not as a people departed far, very far, from the paths of truth and justice, of humanity and true liberty! And should we not reasonably expect the vengence of Heaven to be visited upon us? May God in his Infinite mercy help us to bear our great afflictions with a propper spirit of meekness, knowing that Ere long we may be transported to that World where sorrow is not known.

Dinner is ready so I must close. I am qu[i]te well. There has been heavy cannonading to our right nearly all day. We may have another fight here before long. Appearances rather indicate something of the kind. Excuse the blunders in this awful scrawl. I have not time to read over and make corections. Lt. Shell has tendered his resignation. How does Mr. Smith[4] get along and have you plenty of wood? Ever your own

George

Murfreesboro

Feb. 8th. As I did not Send this out yesterday I will pencil a few lines this Morning. Our regt. was called into line and marched out to the front to reinforce the pickets, as an attack was anticipated, but all is quiet. Last night there was brought in Three Brigadier genrls., Twelve Staff officers, and escort of Some 75 men. They were enforcing the [Confederate] conscript law in the vicinity of Lebanon when a detachment of the 4th Reg. Cavalry surprised and captured the whole party.[5] The fortifications here are being pushed forward with all possible speed. Every thing is being got ready as fast as posable, either for defence or a forward moovement. Which it is I am unable to say, but it is my opi[nion] that Brag is being reinforced and will undertak the task of getting posesn. of Murfreesbor. If that be the case, there will be fought one of the bloodiest Battle[s] of the war. It is quite certain that Brag will not again meet "old Rose" without an overwh[e]lming fo[r]ce, and it is eqally certain that Rosecranz will not leave this place without trial of strength and Generalship. If they should hold off for Ten days moore they may bring Three men to our one, and I should not doubt the result. Brag is reported to have received Forty Thousand reinforcments, which would make his force not less than one hundred thousand men—a force that we could not meet except under cover of fortfications without disastrous results.[6]

We now have a chaplain—a Mr. ———— —an Episcopalian. Very good man I think—usually gives us one sermon every Lord's Day.[7] A kiss to the little folks. Good by. Ever your own

George

1. Regimental historian Rerick called this period "in one respect the darkest of the war, especially to Indiana soldiers." Less than satisfactory results in the field, combined with heightened opposition at home to both the war and the government's war measures, damaged the morale of many men. Antiwar and pro-Confederate organizations such as the Knights of the Golden Circle were believed to be very strong in Indiana and even to control the state legislature. Rerick, *The Forty-fourth Indiana Volunteer Infantry*, 86–89.

2. Clement L. Vallandigham of Ohio was rapidly becoming the best-known antiwar leader in the North. Jesse D. Bright was a longtime Democrat who had represented Indiana in the U. S. Senate for several years prior to the Civil War. He was expelled from that body soon after the war began for being pro-Confederate.

3. Throughout the war, the Confederates pursued the chimerical hope that one or more sections of the North could be induced to withdraw from the Union and hence abandon the war against the South. From time to time, the Rebels dangled various inducements before the Northerners in an effort to bring about such a secession.

4. Smith is unidentified except by the context, which suggests that he is a friend in Indiana.

5. A false camp rumor. Brigadier generals never would have accompanied a small band to enforce the conscript law. The rumor may have evolved from camp talk about a scouting expedition (February 3–5) that captured forty-three Confederates. See *OR*, vol. 23, pt. 2, 42–46. The 4th United States Cavalry Regiment, a unit of the "Regular Army," was in the 1st Brigade, 2d Division, of the army's Cavalry Corps.

6. The report was false. On January 31, 1863, Bragg's army reported 44,205 officers and men present for duty. *OR*, vol. 23, pt. 2, 622–23.

7. Isaac F. Roberts was commissioned regimental chaplain January 10, 1863. He resigned November 7, 1863. The regiment's first chaplain was Green W. Beeks, who resigned December 1, 1862, for reasons of health. Marion Butler (*My Story*, 283) wrote that he "failed entirely to gain the respect and confidence of the boys. . . . He was more of an aristocrat than minister." See also Rerick, *The Forty-fourth Indiana Volunteer Infantry*, 261–62, 277.

LETTER 8

Camp Near Murfreesboro, Tenn. Feb. 19th, 1863

My own Dear Ellen,

Monday morning, bright [and] ear[ly]. Our rgt., including myself, left for Nash-ville as escort for a supply train—rode all the way. I have spoken about the good roads through this neighborhood, but then I knew little of the road as it now is from Nash-ville to Murfreesboro. What was on[c]e a good sollid stone pike is now allmost one dence mass of mud. The road is entirely spoiled by the continual passage of the Heavy Army waggons. For the whole length of the road may be seen carcasses of dead horse[s and] mules, fragments of waggons & gun carriages. Near Lavergne (15 mils. from Murfreesboro) is scores of remains of Waggons, Ambulences, and mules which were burned by Wheeler's Cavalry during the Battle of Stones river.

We arrived at Nashville about sun down on Monday and took up quarters in the court ho[use]. Monday was pleasent overhead but O dear, how awful mudy. Visited Cyrene in the convalescent camp with severel other of the 44th boys. Cyrene is about the same as when he left camp. He complains that he gets no letters from home—has had none since he left the regt. I think it would go rather hard for me to go two months without hearing from you. I presume I should not *die*, but Should certnly feel desperate. A week seems like a long time to await mail, but of cours you can write no oftener. And though I may write every day, you only hear from me once in Seven days. When I think of this, it is certainly seems foolish for me to write as often as I do. But then I get *so* lonely and then nothing will do me so much good as writing to you. I hardly know how I could exist (we don't *live* in the army) were it not for the pleasure of writing and reading your letters. I am sure I cannot tell how often your letters are read and "reread and reread." O, I'd like to see Chat[1] once more. Do you hear from her often? Where is she and is she *married*? And that puts me in mind of Sister Lib[2]—how is she and has Will[3] returned from his European tour?

Well, we staid in Nashville Tuesday night. Wednesday morning we started out through rain and mud, and at night camped at Lavergne, where I found the 14th O[hio]. Saw many of my acquaintens—Sam, Dave, and Jo Bice, I. Donat, Henry Bron, and a host from Antwerp and vicinity.[4] Their regt. has been out severel months longer then ours, and yet they are over Seven Hundred strong, while we have scarsely one Fifth of that number. We have in the 44th for duty from 140 to 155 men. You ask where are they? Where is the one thousand men who less than Eighteen months ago left Camp Allen on that cold and dismal day, a day which you with many others will long remember? Follow up the cours of the regt. since then and the little mounds of Earth which mark its path will account for many, *very* many of those brave fellows. The fire is entirely out of the stove, and I'm getting chilly. And as the town clock just tolled out the hour of 11 (my usual go to sleep time), I must wish you good night and pleasant dreames. But now [that] I think of it, have you been disturbed since the night you fired through the window?[5] And is mother still with you? How I would like to fill this sheet yet tonight. But it [is] getting so awful cold, I *must* "retire to my virtuous couch." So once moore, Dear one, good nigh[t]. Do you remember how long it used to take us to part? Rather later in the night than this—many years since. I do.

20th. I will now finnish this scrawl so that I can send it out by tomorrow's mail. Yesterday and today the weather has been delightfully pleasant. Our camp is nice and dry, and Six months since I could have enjoyed myself here very well. But now, to tell the truth, I am *sick* of soldiering, and consequently time drags heavily along. Not that our government is worth less than Twelve months ago, but when I know that this war [is] carried on for money making and other selfish purposes, [and] when the majority cares not two straws for the government, I certainly do not feel like exposing my life, ruining my health, and enduring all the hardships of military life. You need not fear that I shal so far forget my duty to my family as to desert, but in case of another fight—if there is a chance of "playing out"—I do not know what I may do. One thing is very sure—the day is past when there is any honor to be gained in fighting. But then, what is the use of thinking of the disagreeables of life?

Your No. 12 has arrived. You wanted me [to] give some items of the field after the fight on Monday. After the battle (the reason I did not start out before was that I was so completely worn out I did not care to exert myself any moore than absolutely necessary), I started out to stroll over the scene of the late contest, particulerly where we fought or rather run on Wednesday. In the edge of the open field lay some 50 or sixty of our men who had been carried together, around which there was a rail pen built. There had been rain and the drops of water was standing in their hair, the clothes wet, their glassy eyes stereing one in the face and their dredfuly mutillated bodi[es] was certainly a sickning sight. I [was] perticularly struck with one—a mere boy who had been shot through the heart with [a] musket ball, his pale yet beautiful face [and] long dark hair which was parted and hung in curles and gave him allmost a girlish appeerance. A smile was allmost visible on his open countenance. He died, evidently, without a struggle. We pass along a sho[r]t distance further [and] find another [pen] where was seen the remains [of] an equal number [of] rebbels, one laying on the back with his whole entrails laying on the ground, another with the chest litterly torn to pieces by cannon ball, another with his right shoulder entirly carried away, another with the under jaw torn off. One [had] the top of the head shot away. His brain lay on the ground close by another with both legs shot off close to the body, &c&c. A little further on and near the fence by the woods was a pen containing perhaps Fifteen or Twenty of the 13 O[hio]., brave but unfortunate fellows. Here then, after mont[h]s of toil and hardship, have they found a resting place. To the left was another pen containing a larger number of late enemies. We went through the woods out of which we had once been driven, [a]cross small plantation[s], and come to [the] rebbel hospital, where were hundred[s] of poore fellows, both union and rebbel, who had been carried from the field wounded but had since died. Here were some 15 or 20 men engaged in bur[y]ing the dead. We went down the Franklin pike towards Murfreesboro, pas[t] scors of dead horses and men who had not yet been gathered up. Every little ways we would see a little squad of men bur[y]ing the dead. [We] pas[t] "the brick house" you no doubt have seen mentioned in the papers as being battered to the ground. In the rear of this house is a rebbel bur[y]ing ground, which is evident from the number of hands and feet potruding from the ground. We pass through *that* cotton field where the 9th Indiana done such execution.[6] Here to[o] men were digging holes for the reception of the miserable clay which lay scattered so thick. [We went] over that to the rebbel's fatal field. One place I noticed the boys had dug qu[i]te a deep hole and were pileing the bodies in one on top of the other until nearly level with the surface. Then [they would] press them down in order to get stil *one* more in.

Well, I must close as it would certainly be extravegant to use moore then one sheet, especially of foolscap, for one letter when one writes as often as I do. James Collier[7] sent W.[8] a valentine—did he get it? In your "No. 12" you spoke of writing to Mr. Withers. What for? Be sure and sell the Antwerp lot if you can to any advantage. We have made out four months pay rolls so I shal doubtle[ss] be able to send some money to you, thoug[h] not a[s] much. I shal draw only $40, and you know I owe $10 borrowed money in the regt. ever since I left for home that must be paid and I shal have to use a little. Must have some paper & Envelops and a pair of suspenders, as mine are just about "give out." I will do the best I can for you. Don't know yet how I shal send it home. Good by Dear one. Your loving

George

1. Chat is unidentified except by context.
2. Unidentified except by context, which suggests that she was a sister or sister-in-law of George or Ellen Squier.
3. Unidentified except by context.
4. Samuel, David, and Joseph Bice; Isaac Donat; and Henry A. Brown, all members of Company G, 14th Ohio Infantry Regiment. All five men enlisted on August 26, 1861. Joseph Bice was reported missing on September 19, 1863, at Chickamauga. Brown was killed in action in the same battle. Samuel and David Bice served out their three-year enlistments and were mustered out September 12, 1864. Donat was promoted to corporal December 15, 1863, and to sergeant September 1, 1864. He was mustered out with the company July 11, 1865. The 14th Ohio was in the 2d Brigade, 3d Division, McCook's Wing ("Center") of the army. *Ohio Roster,* vol. 2, 438–39.
5. See Letter 13 in chapter 1 and Letter 11 below.
6. Early in the afternoon of December 31, the 9th Indiana, 2d Brigade, 2d Division, Crittenden's Wing fought against a Confederate assault on the part of the Federal line just north of the Nashville–Murfreesboro road. Hundreds of Confederates were killed or wounded in the attack. See *OR,* vol. 20, pt. 1, 552; Cozzens, *No Better Place,* 161–66.
7. Pvt. James W. Collier, Company D, from Kendallville, was promoted to first lieutenant on June 10, 1863, and dismissed August 13, 1863.
8. "W." is unidentified except by context, which suggests that Squier was referring to his son Wilber.

LETTER 9

Camp near Murfreesboro, Tenn. Apr. 30th, 1863

Very Dear Ellen,

It has been nearly two weeks since the rect. of your last letter. [I] have watched anxiously every day since last Sabbeth but as yet have been each day disappointed. To day there was two papers come, by which I infer that sickness is not the cause of not hearing from you. Perhaps your letter was mislaid. If so, it will doubtless come through in due time. [I] can sympathize with you when you have to wait *two weeks* without hearing from me.

Had a *very* good visit with Cousin "Tip." [We] have been camped within 1 ½ mils. of each other for a long time without knowing but a Thousand mils. separ[a]ted us. He has grown somewhat—is a fine-looking fellow. He is a Sergt. in 25 Ill., do not know what Co.[1] He was wounded at the Battle of Stone river. I wrote to Angeline[2] some time since but have rcd. no answer. There is a great many Indiana soldiers now being discharged through the influence of Gov. Morton. Isn't it unfo[r]tunate that I should get well just as I did? But really I don't feell bad over it. Am not quite as "blue" as two months ago—feel willing to soldier when well, as long as our Dear Country needs my poor services, but it is really a hard place to be sick. Then you perhaps have not fo[r]gotten my dispo[si]tion to look on the dark side of the picture when sick. Thank fortune I am well now and feel like myself once moore.

The weather is very fine. Skirmishi[n]g nearly every day on our extreme right. There is an attack anticipated but I think there is little danger unles Brag can bring an overwhelming force, say one hundred thousand men. Do not know where he could get them without weakening some other important point. They surely cannot be spared from Charleston, Fredricksburgh, nor Richmond, neither from the Gulf and much less from Vicksburgh. So there seems to me (though it is not the general opinion) there is little danger of a fight at this place. Neither would it seem good policy to moov this army further South until the fall of Vicksbu[rg]h or Richmond, which is not likely to take place for sometime to come. It would be a great thing for our cause if we could get possession of the Mississip[pi] river and thus cut off one third of the enemy's territory.

[I] am reelly gratified at the position our government has taken towards Great Brittan. It does not pay to play the supplient, to get down on our knees to "eat dust" to the proud, aristocratic, exacting, unprincipaled Brittan. The soldiers *detest* the English. A very common exp[r]ession is [to] the effect that though tired of soldiering they would enlist another Three years to whip England and annex Cannada to the United States. Don't know what your husband might do in such a case.[3] It is bed time, so good night.

Next morning. A duty done for the day. Mail goes out in short time. We now have Co. cooks. Two men cook for the Co. It is by o[r]der from [the] Medical purveyor of this department. Yesterday was the day set apart by the President for fasting (not feasting) and prayer.[4] We had a sermon in the afternoon and prayer meeting in the evening. Last night our new Major was announced late—Capt. Wilds of 11th Michigan.[5] It does not sound very flattering to the officers of the 44th to [have] a man from another regt. appointed over them, but I have not time to give the reeson now. May some other time. Good by. My love to all. Is Mother with you and did W. get his Inkstand from Jerome[?][6] As ever your affectionate

George

1. "Tip" was probably Sgt. Harrison Goodspeed, Company K, 25th Illinois, 3d Brigade, 1st Division, XX Corps, who was wounded at Stones River. The assumption is that "Harrison" was named for President William Henry ("Old Tippecanoe") Harrison—hence, "Tip." The editors thank Mike Musick of the National Archives for this suggestion.

2. Unidentified except by context.

3. Probably a reference to the 1863 diplomatic spat over the "Laird rams"—powerful warships being built in Great Britain (under clever subterfuges) for the Confederacy. In early 1863, the United States government enacted a "privateering bill" that, if implemented, would have authorized the issuance of letters of marque and reprisal to American vessels. Such privateers would have posed a great danger to British commerce. Almost all ships attempting to enter the blockaded Southern ports were British. Inevitably, the privateers would have at least interfered with British vessels engaged in legitimate commerce with neutral countries. Ships of the Royal Navy would act to protect the British vessels. Sooner or later there would have been a clash between United States and British warships that would have escalated into war. Neither side wanted war and, eventually (in September), the British government seized the rams. Many Federal soldiers resented the pro-Confederate attitude that the British upper classes often seemed to display and the fact that such Rebel vessels as *Alabama* and *Florida* were built in Britain (by private firms) and then escaped to serve the Confederacy. On the complexities posed by the "Laird rams" issue, see John David Smith, "Yankee Ironclads at Birkenhead? A Note on Gideon Welles, John Laird and Gustavus V. Fox," *The Mariner's Mirror,* 67 (February 1981): 77–82.

4. For Lincoln's proclamation designating April 30 as a "day of national humiliation, fasting, and prayer," see Roy P. Basler, ed., *The Collected Works of Abraham Lincoln,* vol. 6 (New Brunswick, N.J., 1953), 155–56.

5. Capt. William M. Wiles had served in the 22d Indiana and on Rosecrans's staff. Although commissioned major of the 44th Indiana, he never served with the unit because he was almost immediately promoted to lieutenant colonel of the 22d Indiana. He had no connection with the 11th Michigan.

6. Unidentified except by context.

LETTER 10

Murfreesboro May 24th, 1863

Dear Ellen,

A letter from Nettie and Pamelia[1] just received dated 12th inst. informes me that our Dear Sister "Lib" is again with you. How much I should like to be at home just a little while during her visit among the friends. It is not worth while to send her any word, as she will have taken her departure before this reaches you. The weather is quite warm, though not *hot* yet. Our great "bore," the very *pest* of our lives which persecute *incessently* and without mercy from the "rising of the Sun to the going down thereof"[2] is flies—common house flies (you remember how I dislike them perhaps). They swarm in myriads wherever you go in the evening or morning. The branches of trees are lined with them, the ground litterly covered, and our tents perfectly black. Scarsely can you get a mouthful of food from the plate to your mouth without having to stop several times and remoove those awful creatures. Imagine yourself eating light bread and tea. There is a piece of the delicacy nicely ballanced on your spoon— *the fly* has not yet left his poluting mark on it. You are anxious to tast[e] the luxury. The spoon is dashed or *cramed* into the mouth. You hear a slight buz for an instant— a crashing of small bones generally—and all is over. Ther is *one* less fly on this mundane sphere. Every thing is covered with them and their "tracks." One m[i]ght as well think of reposing on a downy bed of Bull thistles as of taking an after dinner nap. Night is the only time for rest.

It appears that there is lively times in the Army of the Tenn. Madame Rumor speaks of the fall of Vicksburgh. Would to God it might be so.[3] Had we only men enough now in the field, it seems this war might be soon brought to a close. But it is not so. We must wait. Perhaps the administration is not incompetent, but it has surely signally failed to anticipate great mighty necessitys. They are, in my opinion, to[o] slow. Last Summer after McLel[lan's] defeat there was called out 300,000 men authorized to be raised months before. The result of postponing until that period was [that] the new regts. were forced to take the field undisciplined and not inured to camp life. Consequently thousands and thousands died of fatigue and exposure, and to day finds them scarcely as strong (numerically) as the old regts. In due time the draft was made, but not in time for the fall campaign. Last winter Congress passed the "conscription act." Here it is, allmost midsummer, and the initiatory steps toward enforcing it is scarsely taken. Why so dilatory? Why not be active, energetic, and in season? Why should not the conscrips be thoroughly organized? By the first of August put them in camp in healthy localities through out Ky. and Mo. [and] drill them thoroughly. They will become used to camp life and partially acclimated. Then in Nov. they will be fit for duty. They will [be as fit] as old soldiers of whom something might reasonably be expected. Instead of that, however, it is put off until the last moment, and the scenes of last Fall are to be reneacted.[4]

Don't know whether I wrote you that the baggage of Noncommissioned officers and soldirs are cut down to one hat or cap, two Shirts (I have 4 and shal keep them), one coat jacket or blouse, 2 pr. drawers, 2 pr. socks (have got 4 pr.), one pr. pants, and one pr. Shoes or boots. Allso one w[oo]len blanket, one rubber blanket, and one "purp" tent, which is substanually the same as last Summer. I sent my things home in about the right time, though it is quite uncertain whether they ever get through. If they do, shal be at least $25 "in." If not, shal be about $150 (the exchanges) "out." Had I have kept them, they would undoubtedly have been lost. Write as soon as you know they have come through if ever. Dress parade, so good evening.

We had a very good sermon this evening by our Chaplein. O! Yes, there is a protracted meeting in progress in the 30th Ind. which has been qu[i]te a success. There has been upwards of Three hundred who have turned from the error of their ways, and still they come, a[n]xious to enlist and fight under Prince Emanuel. Surely it is a Glorious work that is going on. The meetings are under the direction of Col. Moody, or the "Fighting Precher."[5] He is said to be smart, of sound judgeme[n]t, and an allmost illimitable control over the minds of men. This influence is not confined to the pulpit, nor to the one subject of religion. I have not heard him, as it is nearly two miles to where the meetings are held.

Your tea holds out remarkably well. Have just commenced on the second paper. "Nettie" sent me a good drawing in her letter. Have not heard from Gustine[?] for several days.[6] He is remooved to the field Hospital in Town. John Collier I understand is very sick.[7] Some time since he was sent to convalescent camp. The last time he was in camp he looked poorly though quite comfo[r]table. The rest of the boys are all right. My love to all the friends, especially our little ones. Good by. Heaven bless and preserve you all is the prayer of

George

1. Nettie and Pamelia are unidentified except by context, but see reference to Pamelia in Letter 13.
2. See Ps. 113:3 and Mal. 1:11.
3. The rumor was false, although Grant and his Army of the Tennessee had driven the defending Confederates into the city and had laid siege to it.
4. Federal policy was to organize new troops into new regiments rather than send them to strengthen old units where they would learn from the veterans. In 1862, the government called for three hundred thousand men ("volunteers"). Only with great effort (including state-level conscription and bounties) were these troops raised. In March 1863, the Federal government enacted a national conscription law making all able-bodied men twenty to forty-five years of age subject to the draft. There was much opposition to the draft calls, the first of which was made in July 1863 and led to antidraft riots, the worst of which took place in New York City. Maj. Gen. George B. McClellan had been defeated and driven away from Richmond, Virginia, in the summer of 1862.
5. Colonel Moody was almost certainly Granville Moody of the 74th Ohio, 3d Brigade, 2d Division, XIV Corps, and a Methodist minister.

6. Private Gustin was probably Pvt. Horace Gustin of Hall's Corners and Company D, who was discharged for disability on June 20, 1863. See Letter 3, chapter 4.

7. Pvt. John W. Collier of Hall's Corners, veteranized and served with the company until September 14, 1865.

LETTER 11

Murfreesboro, Tenn. June 1st, 1863

My Dear Ellen,

It has now been allmost five months (it will be on 7th) since we came to this camp. Five months—how short the time seems, and yet it is nearly one Seventh of the term of enlistment. To look back to the day we came to this camp—it seems such a very little while—only a few days. It seems impossible that we have spent one third of the time since we left Fort Wayne on that cold, disagreeable morning, and which seems an age ago since, in this very place, and yet such is "supposed to be a fact." One year ago day before yesterday (the 29th of May), the evacuation of Corinth was completed. That mighty army which was gathered there is scattered we hardly know where.[1] A small portion of it is here, not as far South as then by one hundred and fifty miles. But no one can doubt but that we have made *some* progress towards crushing this mighty demon of rebellion. The "boys" are generally rather down hearted at the news from Grant's army, though it appears there is yet slight prospects that they may yet accomplish their work.[2] The Soldiers seldom get jubilent over *reported* victories. They have been disappointed to[o] often to credit every rumor that happens to be set afloat. We wait with something of impatience the result of Gen. Grant's opperations before Vicksburg. Yesterdy I was favored with a letter from friend Webber.[3] He was "all right" and apparently in good spirits. Do you know whether there is any prospects of his being connected with our family! Charlotte never writes any thing about him. The weather is very fine after several days rain. My health is excellent. This is Monday, the day that is allways looked forward to with pleasure, as with it usualy comes tidings from home.

Later. The mail has come in and brought me a letter, but not *the letter.* It was from Sister L., written at home and mailed at Fort Wayne. She says you are all well, which was some satisfaction, though it does not fill the bill. If we stay here until tomorrow doubtless I shal get a letter that will satesfy me for a week. We have orders to ma<r>ch tomorrow morning at 4 o'clock. Where, of course, we can only conjecture. In case of Grant's success I have expected a moovement on Talahoma [Tullahoma] and perhaps Chatanooga. Of course, this is only my opinion, the reason for which I think I have given in some of my former letters. Did not Mr. Neall and Mr. Burrier[4] feel rather cheep while being overhauled by the P.G. [Provost Guard] of Indianapolis! I understand that Burrier was relieved of a very fine revolver and various other things. If it is so I say good! If some of those copper heads[5] were relieved of their *wind* for the space of fifteen or twenty minutes it might be the means of their seeing the error of their ways. Do you know whether Father and Lafayette goes armed? I hope not. It does not look well for peaceable citizens *staying at home* to go armed to the teeth (I do not mean women—you know that would be comeing rather close [to] home).[6]

If we should now be about entering on an active campaign, I may not be able to write regularly. If you do not hear from me as often as once a week, it will be because it is impossable for me to write, and I would like to have you continue to write as often as once a week. I will agree to do the best I can. It will be best to sell the Antwerp lot if you can get $150 for it, and [do] with the money as you think best. Perhaps it will be best to let Netherpose[?][7] have our or rather *your* place if he will pay a fair cash rent. How much live stock—not including the children—have you got? Better dispose of all you can to advantage. Cattle are so liable to die. Besides, they are necessarily some trouble to you and I would have you get along wi<th as> little care as possable. And above all things, *don't work to[o] hard.* Better let the work go undone than kill yourself doing it.

To day we drew p[e]r man two pound potatoes and half pound dried apples, for which we are indebted to the Sanitery commission.[8] We have soft bread all the time now. We draw from the Q.M. [Quartermaster] two days out of five. With the company fund I get flour at $6.35 p[e]r bbl. for which the baker furnishes us with all the bread we need. I need not tell you we live *well,* perhaps to[o] well for *soldiers.* They should have only hard tack, Sow belly, and coffee. Give them as few of the comforts of life as possable. But it is allmost dark so good night dear one. May Heaven bless and preserve you all is the daily prayer of your ever loveing

George

1. The Confederate army that fought at Shiloh retreated twenty miles southwest to Corinth, Mississippi. After evacuating that post at the end of May 1862, it moved via Mobile, Alabama, and Chattanooga, Tennessee, into east-central Kentucky. When forced back by Buell's army, it took up a position at Murfreesboro, Tennessee. Early in 1863, the Confederates retreated to the Tullahoma area, where they were posted in June 1863. Squier, however, refers to the vast Union force that moved from Shiloh to Corinth. After Corinth fell, part of it under Grant went to the Mississippi Valley. Another part under Buell moved eastward toward Chattanooga but had to hasten northward to meet the Rebels in Kentucky. Other parts were scattered about to garrison various captured towns.

2. Grant was still besieging Vicksburg. By June 1, the Yankees in Tennessee had probably learned of the bloody and unsuccessful attack that Grant had made on the city's fortifications on May 22. In these attacks, Grant lost 3,200 men and gained nothing.

3. Webber is unidentified except by context.

4. Neall and Burrier are unidentified except by context. Squier clearly believed them to be Confederate sympathizers.

5. "Copperhead" was the derisive term used to refer to those Northerners (usually Democrats) who opposed the Federal government's war policies and who believed that it would be possible, even easy, to negotiate an agreement with the Confederates that would both

halt the war and restore the Union. Most Federal soldiers despised them. The Lincoln administration sought to suppress their activities by censorship of the press, arrests, and other means.

6. See Letter 13 in chapter 1 and Letter 8 above.
7. Unidentified except by context.
8. The U.S. Sanitary Commission was a civilian organization formed to improve soldiers' lives by providing special food and other items beyond those the government issued to the troops. It also helped to care for the sick and wounded and provided meals and sometimes sleeping quarters for transient soldiers.

LETTER 12

Murfreesboro, Tenn. June 8, 1863

Dear Ellen,

Your supposed to be No. 30 is just rcd. I was very sorry to hear that you are so very poorly. Do, I beg of you, take a good long rest. Go out to Farmer and make a real visitation. Stay as long as you can. Enjoy yourself visiting among your numerous friends and acquaintences. You might let Lafayett's folks have the cow to milk and take care of in your absence. You have no other live stock that claims your attention, I believe. I can see nothing to hinder your staying away two or three mont[h]s or even longer if you choose. If you should go, let me know and I will write to some of the Farmer folks every week so that you can hear from me as often as when at home. [I] will allso continue to write to you at Halls Corners, so you will in either case hear from me as often as usual. For fear or rather in hopes you may go out there, I perhaps had better write to them rather often until I hear from you again. Don't know that there is any thing for me to say that has not allready been written about your working so hard. For pity sake, for your own sake, for the sake of your children and for my sake, do take the rest so necessary for your health. You did not say whether you had received the box of things which you said in No. 25 was at Comparetts. I would like to know whether they went through all right. There was nothing of any great value in the box, but stil I would not like to have them lost. The rubber blanket is new and will doubtle[ss] come [in] very handy.

This morning we rec[e]ived orders to "fix up"—that is, clean our guns, brush clothes, black shoes, &c&c. And what was all this fuss for? Only to see one of the 55th O.V.I. [Ohio Volunteer Infantry] boys shot for desertion. The order was countermanded. The man is not to be shot at present. A petition is being sent up for his reprieve. There is allso one of the 86 Ind. under sentence of death for the similar offence. Both of those regts. are in the 6th Brigade. Whether either will [be] executed, it is impossible to tell. Things begin [to] "tighten" in the discipline of this army, as well as among the Copperheads up north. There appears to be no news from the army of the Tennessee. Only Grant is pegging away, apparently confident of success. I cannot but feel anxious about the result of his opperations. There is doubtless some great moovement on the part of the enemy. His removal from the Rapahennock is not for nothing. There is doubtless a blow to be struck some where. It would hardly seem probable [that] they will give up Virginia after so long and arduous a struggle to hold it. Yet, in my opinion, they (the rebbels), better give up Virginia than loose the Mississippi river. With the loss of that stream goes one half of the so-called Southern Confederacy. If Port Hudson and Vicksburgh be reduced, all of Mississ[ippi] and most of All. [Alabama] will very soon be in our posses[si]on, and the rebellion virtually crushed. It will be moore for our interest to reduce port Hudson and Vicksburgh than Richmond and, in fact, all of Virginia. There will be no moovement here until one advance on the part of either Grant or Hooker.[1] Will not this do for the present for my opinion on war matters? I think so.

The weather is fair, with cold nights. We have very good preaching *of the kind* every Lord's Day by our chaplain, a very good man whom I esteem very highly. He appears to do all he can to awake an interest in religion, but so far with little apparent effect. There appea[r]s even among pro[fe]ssing Christians, and your husband among the rest, a lack of vitality, of that all-absorbing interest which should characterize the life [of] every Christian under all circumstances. I feel the lack of someth[in]g, but fail to apply the propper remedy. Love to all, your self included, and kiss for Wilber, Allice, and our dear little pet Ella.

George

1. Port Hudson, Louisiana, was some three hundred river miles down the Mississippi River from Vicksburg. It was then under siege by Union forces that had moved upriver from the Baton Rouge area. In June 1863, the Confederates in Virginia were beginning the maneuvers that would lead to the Battle of Gettysburg. They did so, in part, in an effort to draw Grant away from Vicksburg. Maj. Gen. Joseph Hooker then commanded the Federal army in Virginia.

LETTER 13

Murfreesboro, Tenn. June 11th, '63

Dear Ellen,

Having a little leisure just now will commence the second letter for this week. You know I rather make it a point to write twice a week. The mail has just come in with the *report* of the surrender of Vicksburgh. We hardly dare indulge in the hope that it is correct.[1] Night before last we had a very fine time, a real feast. Ex-Lt. Gov. "Billy Williams"[2] from Kociusko [Kosciusko], Ind., a fine union man though a life long democrat, addressed the 44th and 86th I.V.I. on the subjects now agitating the public mind. Perhaps an act. [account] of the meeting might not be uninteresting, allso of the speach so far as my memory serves me. The [lieutenant governor] assended the stand or rather the army wagon in company with Lt. Col. Aldrich,[3] who introduced him in something like the following: "soldiers of the army of the Cumberland, permit me to introduce to [you] my old friend from Indiana, Gov. Billy Williams, who is a gentleman and a scholar who has but one failing—that of a bad breaking out at the mouth." After three rousing cheers for the Gov., he arose and after a few compliments to soldiers in general and those present in particuler, he briefly refered to the revolutionary struggle, the labors and exposurs of the fathers of this republic. He spoke of the mighty Empire grown up so suddenly on the foundations laid by those great and good men. We have lived and prospered for moore than fifty years in peace and quietude. Finaly a dark and lowering cloud arose in the south which spread and covered our fair land. He contrasted the administration of the imbecil bachelor President[4] with that of Gen. Jackson, who would have hu[n]g a traitor on every Palmetto tree in South Carolina.[5] He refered to the secretary, Floyd Swindle[6]— he could see him on his journey to Washingto[n] after his appointment by *"James Buchenon"*. He could hear him saying in the language of the old methodist hymn, "This is the way I long have sought, and mourned because I found it not," and South Carolina, continuing, "If you get there before I do, Look out for me I'm coming to[o]."[7] Mr. Lincoln had made some mistake[s], had done *some* things which in His (the speake[r]'s) opinion, [he] ought not to have done but doubtless he (the President) would not have done it if he (the speaker) had told him that it was not policy. He took his seat in peculiar circumstances, with seven states allready procl[a]imed out of the union, with civil war inauegrated, with an empty treasurey, with the arms and munitions of war stolen and in the hands of the enemy, with every department filled with scoundrels and traito[r]s. Yet in two yeers he has raised, armed, and equiped an army of a million of men, built a navy that defies the world, effectually block-aded over two thousand miles of sea coast—and all this without incurring a debt to any foregn power. Never in the history of the world has there been so much accom-plished in so short [a] time. He spoke of the confiscation act and the howl set up by the despicable sympathizers that it was *unconstitutional*.[8] But they never had a word of condemnation for Jef Davis and his bogus congress, who have confiscated moore than two millions of property of union men in the south, who have hung many for the hanous crime of loyalty, and exiled defenceless women and children.[9] The sus-pension of the writ of habeas corpus next claimed his attention. Its suspension did [not] effect loyal men, and should we be so careful of the interests of traitors,[10] asked whether Gen. Jackson in like action was not sustained, that the Great Douglas pre-sented a bill to Congress refunding to the heirs of Gen. Jackson the fine of one thou-sand dollars, imposed for the *crime* of imprisoning traitors.[11] The proclimation was conclusive evidence to the copperheads that this is an oppressive, unjust, and unholy war urged fo[r] the abolition of slavery. God sent Jonah to the Ninevehans and com-manded him to proclaim yet forty days and Nineveh shal be des[t]royed. They were alarmed at the proclimation of the Allmighty. They gave up their idols, they repented in sack cloth and ashes, and their city was spared.[12] Abraham Lincoln gave the Idola-trous rebbels *one hundred days* of grace. They repented not, and their mighty city, their wors than haram, their darling inst[it]ution must fall.[13] [It] is allready to fling over into the abys of Eternal infamy. He denounced the copperheads in scathing terms. He said that if Vicksburgh and port Hudson should surrender, three-fourths of the men who now repudiate the President, the war, and every thing else but *Democracy* would *swear* that they *allways had* been in favor of a vigorous prosecution of the war. When you get home there will not be a man who ever has felt sympathy for the rebbels. They always have been warm advocates for the war and the policy of the administration. He was often interrupted by cheers, c[l]apping of hands, &c. The band gave us "rally round the flag" when Maj. Martin[14] was called to the stand. He made a few pertinent remarks on the duty of the soldir. If Vicksburgh and Port Hudson should fall, the war would close in Ninty days. The band then played yanke[e] doodle when Capt. Otis[15] was loudly called for by the crowd. He arose and s[a]id he had a few words to say to the Hon[o]rable gentleman who had so nobly spoken to us to night. He should tell the Citizens of Indiana that their unbounded confidence in the army of the Cumberland was not *entir[ely]* misplaced. When we mooved, it would be to victory. That we would never give up while there was an armed traitor in the land. When we have whiped the south, we would return North and have a reckon[ing] with those miserable butternuts. There is not a soldier in this entire army who has not marked his man or men in his own vicinity. The day is not far distant when they will call for the hills and mountains to fall on them to hide them from the wrath that has overtaken them. He then proposed three cheers for "Old Rose" and his purps, which was given with a right good will. When the meeting broke up, the band playing "Dixie," every man left the spot feeling himself a stronger man than when he came. If you wish to keep an army in good spirits, favor them with good speakers and lady visitors from home, ladies who do not devote their entire attention to the officers. We often hear the soldiers say "God bless the ladies of the sanitary commission." They are certainly doing a great de[a]l for the comfort of the soldiers in camp.

Howell[?] is in hospital.[16] My health is first-rate, the weather decidedly cool for this climate at this season of the year. In fact, it is rather cool for a moore northern latitude. Is it not fortunate for the poor fellows at Vicksburgh and port Hudson; it will be the means of saving thousands of lives and prevent a great deal of suffering.

The term "Old Rose's purps" may need a little explanation. Some two months since all the [Sibley] and [Bell?] tents[17] were turned over to the QM and the shelter tents issued which is coarse, heavy muslin about 6 x 5 feet. Two of these put together make a shelter for the men which the boys call a purp tent.

Well, I think this will do for quantity; the quality I will say nothing about. I was very much interested and amused with the speachifying but I know the accou[n]t is not as much so. Perhaps it may be rather a bore than otherwise. If so, there is nothing lost moore than your time of reading it. My time when I have leisur is not very valuable. I have once or twice to write to Lafayette but have received no answ[er]. Sister Charlotte has not written for a long time. In regard to my correspondence with T. Powell,[18] do not imagine that our letters are very close together. She wrote me, I answered, and wishing to hear from the friends in Farmer occasionally, and she being the first one of them to write, I have since kept up the correspondence. In fact, she is the only one (except in her last Pamelia put in a few words) who has fav[or]ed me with a line. When I get a letter from her I answer it and the same with her. Consequently, our letters are far between but often cross.

I had not spac[e] on the first page to say good by so I will say it now.

George

1. The report was false.

2. This refers to William Williams of Warsaw, Kosciusko County, Indiana, who never served as lieutenant governor of the state but was nominated for that office in 1852 by the Whigs. He had commanded Camp Allen at Fort Wayne and then served as an army paymaster. A Republican after 1860, Williams served in the U.S. House of Representatives 1867–75 and as chargé d'affaires in Paraguay and Uruguay 1882–85.

3. Lt. Col. (later Col.) Simeon C. Aldrich of Pleasant Lake was originally captain of Company K. He was commissioned lieutenant colonel December 6, 1862, and colonel July 27, 1863. He died at home August 15, 1864, of disease.

4. A reference to President James Buchanan (1857–61). Many Northerners indicted Buchanan for what they considered to be his timid, pro-South conduct in the late 1850s and in the secession crisis of 1860–61. They believed that his vacillating conduct permitted, if not encouraged, the Southern states to secede.

5. President Andrew Jackson (1829–37) took a tough stand against an attempt by South Carolina to "nullify" a Federal tariff law in the late 1820s and early 1830s.

6. John B. Floyd of Virginia, Buchanan's secretary of war, was widely believed by Northerners to have been especially corrupt. They accused him of using his cabinet post to help the South prepare for rebellion by shipping large quantities of weapons to sites in the South prior to the war.

7. These quotations derive from "River of Jordan" in John G. McCurry, *The Social Harp*, eds. Daniel W. Patterson and John F. Garst (1855; reprint, Athens, 1973), 21; "Swing Low, Sweet Chariot," in *The United Methodist Hymnal: Book of United Methodist Worship* (Nashville, 1989), 703.

8. Probably a reference to the law of August 6, 1861, that authorized seizure of property used to aid the Confederacy. It is possible that Williams referred to the "Second Confiscation Act," which became law July 17, 1862—or to both pieces of legislation. The latter law specifically stated that slaves belonging to persons in rebellion would become free once they entered Union lines.

9. It is uncertain what Williams meant by this accusation. The Confederate government never embarked on an official program of confiscating the property of Unionists. Williams may have referred to some action by a Confederate state or local government, or he may simply have been repeating Northern propaganda. On occasion (as in Texas and eastern North Carolina), some local authorities or military commanders hanged persons who were—or were suspected of being—Unionists.

10. At various times, Lincoln, by proclamation, suspended the writ of habeas corpus in dif-

ferent parts of the country, usually to the accompaniment of howls from both Confederate sympathizers and loyalists sincerely concerned about civil liberties.

11. Early in 1815, near the end of the War of 1812, Gen. Andrew Jackson declared martial law in New Orleans. He arrested and exiled from the city a judge who tried to overrule him. When news of the peace treaty reached the city soon afterward, Jackson lifted martial law. The judge then returned, ruled Jackson in contempt of court, and fined him $1,000. Jackson paid the fine. Thirty years later, the Federal government remitted the money to the general's heirs. Stephen A. Douglas, a former judge and then a member of the House of Representatives from Illinois, played a prominent role in securing enactment of the necessary legislation. See Robert V. Remini, *Andrew Jackson and the Course of American Empire, 1767–1821* (New York, 1977), 308–15.

12. See Jon. 3–4.

13. Lincoln's preliminary Emancipation Proclamation had stipulated that emancipation would not apply to slaves in states that abandoned the rebellion by January 1, 1863.

14. Martin is unidentified other than by context. He may have been William H. Martin of the 93d Ohio, 3d Brigade, 2d Division, XX Corps, who had been promoted to lieutenant colonel in March.

15. Possibly Capt. E. A. Otis, assistant adjutant general on Van Cleve's staff.

16. Unidentified except by context.

17. Sibley tents were large shelters in which as many as a dozen men could sleep.

18. Unidentified except by context.

LETTER 14

Camp on Stones River, Tenn. June 29, '63

My very Dear Ellen,

Your second letter written at brother D.'s[1] is just received. Was glad to hear that your health is improoving. Now when you get home do not overwork yourself again. Think I have said all I can say on this to me important subject in some of my former letters. Allso explained why I did not write to you at Farmer.

The fight goes bravely on, but you will get the details per Telegraph long ere this reaches its destination. In fact, we get but little reliable news from the front. Every thing in the line of news appears to be suppressed. We have had a great [deal] of rain for a week past, which will be the means of saving many, very many lives of the poor wounded fellows. [We] have not had a warm day since the fight commenced.[2] In fact, it has been first rate fighting weather. Men can endure exposure to rain and cold much better than [to] heat and thirst. There is wounded coming in every day, though not in large numbers. The 21st Corps (ours) lost very heavily a few days since. They were crosing a field, in front of which was heavy timber with thick undergrowth, when nearly across the field and in sho[r]t musket range of the woods the enemy, which had lain concealed in the brush, raised up and poured a murderous fire into our (I me[a]n our men not ourselves as we were far away) ranks, killing the men by scores.

The line wavered and was about [to] retreat when Gen. Critenden (God bless him) dashed in front of his allmost vanquished line, and in the greatest danger he said "fellow soldiers do not forsake me *now*; who will follow me?" Those few words decided the day. At that point, with an unearthly yell, they followed their gallant l[e]ader, charged the rebbels, and drove them from their position. A short sentence, even a *word* spoken in the right time by the right individual, may decide the fate of thousands or even a nation. Last night [at] 11 o'clock our regt. was called out to guard some 400 prisoners who had just arrived from the front. There has been some [?] during the day and so to night the camp of the 44th is *not* held but holds up six hundred of Wheeler's cavalry. They are principal[y] from All., stout, hardy-looking fellows, though quite indifferently clothed. There is no uniformity in their dress. Their woollen blank[ets] are poor excuses, and *no* rubber blankets. Most of them are in good spirits, and confident of the final success of the Southern Confederacy. I was talking with quite an intelligent man about the condition of his army. He said that it was now better clothed and better fed than ever before, [and] that the Northern sympat[hizers] were as much despised in the Southern army as in the Northern.

To day['s] report says that Gen. Rosecrans' head quarters is in Talahoma. Certain it is that the baggage trains have been ordered to Shelbyville, which is a very good sighn that things are mooving along satisfactingly. My health is very good. The mail goes out in a short time, so I must close. Give my love to all and remember me as ever your loving

George

Enclosed you will find a note on Burkey Sheffer[3] which his father promised to pay when I was at home. Will you hand it to Calvin[4] to collect? If Shefer pais it C. can pay the money to you and then you can inform me of the fact.

G.

1. Unidentified. Probably a brother or brother-in-law of George or Ellen Squier.
2. On June 23, Rosecrans advanced from the Murfreesboro area against Bragg's army, which was based at Tullahoma. Crittenden's corps was the left element of the Federal advance. By skillful maneuvering, Rosecrans threatened Bragg's line of supply and forced the Confederates to fall back to Chattanooga. Although the Tullahoma campaign was marked by frequent skirmishes, there was no major battle. By the end of June, Bragg was in rapid retreat for Chattanooga. Van Cleve's division remained at Murfreesboro to garrison that town. On July 7, the division marched for McMinnville, which it occupied on the ninth.
3. Burke D. Shaffer, a corporal in Company D, was from Harlan. He was killed at Shiloh on April 6, 1862.
4. Unidentified except by context, which indicates he was a friend or relative in Indiana.

LETTER 15

For Ellen Squier

McMinnville, Tenn. Aug. 17th, '63

My Very Dear Wife,

The Army of the Cumberland is again in motion, nor will it stop until the rebbel shold, Chatanooga, is thronged with "blue coats." There *may* be many days hard fighting, though it is the general opinion that Brag will follow up his old System of fighting, which you know is running. Chatanooga is a very important point to rebbels, as it will allso be to the Fedrals if once in our possession, and its evacuation will but demonstrate the fact that Brag does not care again to meet the ever victorious Rosecrans. It is my opinion that the rebs have not forgotten the lesson learnd at Stone river, and that on the aproach of our forces they will Skedaddle and perhaps fall back on Atlanta, Geo. The 1st & 3rd Br[i]gade of our division left here yesterday A.< M.>, taking the Sparta road.

18th. Yesterday was the day for mail from Halls Corners, but none came. Neither has ther been any tidings from ther to day. I did not intend finishing this until the rct. of yours, but have got tired of waiting and as there is a probability of our leaveing here in a few days. So for fear I may not have anoth[er] opportunity of writing for [awhile] I will close this up.

O! Yes, I came near forgetting to mention a very important Era in the history <of> the occupat[ion] of the City of McMinnville. Last Monday, a young lady, a refugee from East Tennessee, peraded our streets on horse back, which created quite a stir among the "boys."[1] Not that ladies are so very scarc here that a single one should attract so much attention, but the manner of her dress, which was truely rather novel. Perhaps a discription thereof may interest you. On her head she wore a blue velvet cap encircled with Silver stars, which glittered like diamonds in the sun. Above the pointed piece was a metalic Spread Eagle. Her veil of very fine material was our national collors—red, white, & blue—with the full number of stars in the lower left-hand corner. She wore a dress of white muslin, over which w[as] a riding skirt of alternate stripes of red, whi<te>, and blue. Her apron which was short had in one corner a spread Eagle worked with silk, the work of her own hands. She wore a set of jewelry which migh[t] have made a small fortune—gold bracelets, gold pin, and one finger ring, but no ear "dinglets." She allso carried a small baner attached to an old parasol stock. So you can see it is no wonder she brot down cheers and generel exclamation of appr[oval].

The weather is rather warm, my health neve[r] better. By the by, I have about concluded not [to] accept a commission in the colo[re]d brigade, so if I live you may looke for me home in about twelve or fifteen months.[2] There is little of interest transpireing and my ideas as you will readily belive are decidedly dull, so I will "bring these few lines to a close." My love to all. Remember me to our little ones and write often, will you Ellen, to your own

George

1. East Tennessee was a rabidly anti-Confederate region and many Unionists were forced to flee from there in the early months of the war. A Federal column from Kentucky moved into east Tennessee in late August and occupied Knoxville on September 2.
2. His original three-year term of service was set to expire on November 22, 1864. By accepting a commission in a regiment of the United States Colored Troops units, Squier would have been obligated to remain in service beyond that date (see Letter 17). As it turned out, he extended his term of service ("veteranized"), by accepting a commission as a first lieutenant in the 44th Indiana, and thus remained in service until the regiment was mustered out in the fall of 1865.

LETTER 16

Five miles East [of] Chatanooga, Ten. Sept. 22nd, 1863[1]

Dear Ellen,

Once moore have I passed through the firey o[r]deal (litterally) of another three days fight and come out without serious injury. I have no chance of giving the particulars of our part in the hardest fought battle that the American continent has ever seen. Nor is it yet ended. We came to this place yesterday evening and are stationed here to guard one of the approaches to Chatanooga. On Fri[day the] 18th we were attacked by the combined forc[e]s of Brag, Buckner, Johnson with his paroled men who have not yet been exchanged, Longstreet with Forty-Three thousand men, A.P. Hill's & Ewel's Corps. In all, according to statements of Prisoners, not less than 140,000 men.[2] But I have time [to] write but very little. I was struck on the leg with [a] spent ball, but [it] done no serious damage, only making me rather lame. There was hard fighting in front yesterdy, the result of which is not known. There is one thing very sure—unless reinforcments come up, we must sur[e]lly loose the day. My health is very good, though I am completely worn out. The loss of our regiment is about 75 men.[3] Good by. Ever your own George. I don't know as you can read this.

G.W. Squier

1. Rosecrans moved against Chattanooga in late August. By crossing the Tennessee River southwest of the city, he threatened the Confederates' supply line and forced the Rebels to evacuate the city on September 6. Rosecrans then pushed on into north Georgia, where the reinforced secessionists pounced on him at Chickamauga (September 18–20). Defeated, the Federals fled back to Chattanooga.
2. Confederate generals who fought in Bragg's army at Chickamauga included Maj. Gen.

(later Lt. Gen.) Simon B. Buckner, whose troops from east Tennessee reinforced Bragg, and Lt. Gen. James Longstreet, who brought some twelve thousand reinforcements to Bragg from Virginia. Gen. Joseph E. Johnston, commanding in Mississippi, sent troops to aid Bragg but did not himself go to Georgia. The Federals maintained that Johnston's men had been captured at Vicksburg, paroled (released on a promise not to fight again until exchanged), and sent to fight in Georgia, although not yet exchanged. The Confederate government had declared them exchanged. Lieutenant generals Ambrose P. Hill and Richard S. Ewell served in Virginia. Neither they nor any of their troops were at Chickamauga. Bragg's strength at Chickamauga was about sixty-six thousand.

3. The 44th Indiana rendered valuable service in the Battle of Chickamauga, losing 72 of its 229 men. Aldrich's report of his unit's role in the battle is in *OR,* vol. 30, pt. 1, 827–29.

LETTER 17

Chattanooga, Tenn. Oct. 2nd, 1863

My Dear Wife,

I had intended giving you the details of the battle as far as came under my observation, but on looking over my notes (not Green backs),[1] they are so very similar to that of Stone River only *moore* so, that it will hardly interest you. But if you wish it let me know and you shal be accommodated at my earliest convenience. It may not be amiss to say that the 44th in every instance behaved well [and] fought splendidly; that it has lost none of its reputation as a fighting regiment, though we done three day's hard fighting and one day's skirmishing. Our regt. only lost Seventy-three in killed and wounded. Of that number, five is of Co. D, all wounded. Of your acquantances is Ezra and Ira Worden, both of which "stood up to work" bravely.[2] They have not been heard from since they left the field. I have not yet seen a statement of our loss, but think it cannot fall much sho[r]t of Twenty Thousand men in killed, wounded, and missing.[3] There is one thing very sure—that Stone River was a play spell, a mere Skirmish compared with the battle of Chckamauga (not Chickamauga as formerly written). The boys thought they knew what suffering [was] before this fight, but they never did.

On Friday night, Sept. 18th, our regt. lay in front. It was a cold night. We could make no coffee for supper, nor fire at night. There was neither blanket nor overcoat. [We] were very tired and had to lay there shivering on the cold ground all night long. I shook from head to foot as though I had a fit of ague, and O how I wished that it was the case, for then I knew it would be followed by the heat of fever. But we lived through it and at sunrise were mooved to the reer, where we had fires and soon each set down to drink a cup of hot coffee, after which we felt much better.

It would now be a very easy and not unpleasant task to give you the details of *our* part of the mig[h]ty contest which raged through Saturdy and Sunday, but I will desist.[4] On Sunday there was great suffering for want of water. I started in with canteen full. I used it very speringly, but some [of] the boys had no canteens, others neglected to go 2 ½ mils. to fill theirs in the morning, so [by] noon my canteen was empty. At 2 [I] was very thirsty; at three I thought myself allmost famishing; and at 4 P.M. would have given all my Earthly possessions (though that wouldn't be much would it?) for [a] single draught of cold water. At dark we mooved off the field, and after walking two mile[s] found a *mud* hole. But that water thick as *gruel was better than any which I ever drank.*

Well, we are now snugly in camp about one mile from town up the river. We occupy the front line or the first ditch. The enemy is directly in f[r]ont in plain view, that is, their camp fires, waggons, and horsemen. Our pickets are about 300 yds. apart. There is now but little fireing along the lines. There is two rebbel sharp shooters which our boys call "long Tom" and "Lumber Jim," which annoys the officers and stragling men considerably if not moore. If an officer or man without his gun steps out in sight, he is sure to be greeted with a ball whistleing past his head. The sentinels that walk up fearlessly to their post is not disturbed, but let one act a little *skeery,* dodg at every little noise, &c, and whiz a ball will go far over his head or strike the ground at his feet. The man of course dodges *some,* and then he is greeted with a loud boisterous la[u]gh from "Long Tom." When our boys shoot at him, he only turns insultingly on them.

On the 29th ult. there wa[s] an arrangement entered into betwe[e]n Gens. Rosecrans and Bragg for the perole of wounded prisoners. Accordingly, on the 30th, 29–3[0] ambulances were sent out with flag of truce as far as the ene[m]y's line. The drivers were there put under guard and "secesh" drivers take the teams, load up the ambulances, and drive bak to the lines in this way.

There has been about three thousand men shot in within four days. They say that the battle field is now an awful sight. But few of the dead on either side are buried, and of cours by this time must be in a high state of decomposition. My health is very good. If Father should come down here this Fall (I don't expect him now as we are so far from R. R. [railroad]), I don't know that I need anything in the line of clothing. Can get drawers (cotton ones) of the Government as cheap as they can be had at home. I have two good woollen shirts [and] one cotton one besides two under shirts that I got from home a year ago. Have not yet had on those stockings you sent me last Spring. Should we have a Winter camp[aign], [I] shal really need a pr. of boots, so I will send my measure[ments]. Have them made of good kip, not to[o] heavy uppers but heavy half double soles, well-nailed on the bottoms.

Your No. 10 written at John's[5] was received day before yesterdy and would have been answered yesterdy, but it rained all day, the first for the past month [?]. It is clear and plesant. The *hot* season is over, thank fortune. O! Yes, I came near forgetting to answer your letter after all. I can hardly imagine how the Idea that I was a Lt. got afloat, as I am *not,* nor is there now any probability of my becoming one, as there is no va[ca]ncy in our co. to be filled. One reason why I did not accept—not a collored commission but a commission in [a] collored regt.—is that they are to serve from three to five years, and I had made up my mind that at the expirat[ion] of my present term of enlistment to at least make a visit among the friends at home. This may seem like a triflering reason, but it certainly has some weight with me. I have written to John and Melissa[6] twice since the rect. of their last. Lomira has not written for a long time. I recd. a letter from sister Charlotte some two week[s] ago which I must certainly answer today.

Give my love to all the friends and write often will you to your own

George

Cane seed from Sequacha valley for Wilber.
The seed sent from Chattanooga valley is allso for W.

1. "Greenbacks" was a term used for some of the "notes" or paper money issued by the Federal government during the war.
2. Like Ezra, Ira Worden, a private in Company D, was from Hall's Corners. He died June 25, 1864, in the Confederate prisoner-of-war camp at Andersonville, Georgia.
3. Federal casualties at Chickamauga were reported at 1,657 killed; 9,756 wounded; and 4,757 missing. Total: 16,170. *OR,* vol. 30, pt. 1, 179.
4. Aldrich's report covering the regiment's role in the battle appears in *OR,* vol. 30, pt. 1, 827–29.
5. John is unidentified except by context. See below in the letter for "John and Melissa." It is unknown if this second reference is to the same man.
6. Unidentified except by context. It is not known if this is the same John referred to above.

Letter 18

Chattanooga Oct. 10th, 1863

My Own Dear Ellen,

We are stil here in what was once the Rebbel strong hold, the key to the heart of the southern confederacy, a point of really moore importance than Richmond. Unless they succeed in holding us in check at this point (they have allready checked us but whether they hold the army now gathering remains to be told), the Southern Confederacy must soon "play out." When I say soon I mean in the cours of two or three years. My opinion is that the great battle of the war will be fought within twenty miles from this place. We are allready reinforce[d] by two corps from the eastern army—the 11th (Segall's old corps), commanded by Maj. Gen. Howard, and the 12th, commanded by Gen. Slocum. There is allso one co[r]ps of Grant's army reported in supporting distance.[1] The rebbels are said to be concentrating a large army in our front. If that be so, another great battle is not far distant.

The reorganization of the army has comenced. The 21st and 20th, Critenden's and McCook's Corps, are consolidated. The 2nd and 3rd divisions are consolidated, commanded by Gen. Wood. Allso the old 2nd [and] 3rd brigades form one (3rd) commanded by Brig. Gen. Beate [Beatty], formerly Col. of 19th O.V.I. [Ohio Volunteer Infantry]. Gen. Van Cleave commands the post at Murfreesboro. So much for new arrangements.[2] It is not yet known whether the decimated regiments will be consolidated. The Eastern boys feel rather "set up" that they are called on to help the much boasted of Western army. This our boys cannot stand, and many is the knock down between the "Western Soldier" and the "Eastern pimp."[?] To help the matter along, the Eastern troops put "some stile"—are finer dressed and appear to think that they are *"some,"* which of course does not go down with our boys. O! Yes, this puts me in mind of the report of deserters from Br[a]gg's army—that the Virginians and a portion [of] Br[a]gg's troops, mostly Kentuckians and Tennesseans, had a pitched battle on 5th inst., in which there was over Six hundred men killed.[3] Deserters are comeing every day. Yesterday a capt. and Lt. with their whole Co. came in. They say their whole Brig. will come in as soon as they are put on out post to give them a chance. The general orders from [the] war department conserning the treatment of such of the confederate army as come voluntarily within our lines is being distributed among the rebs. In this way, the exchange of papers being ve[r]y common, copies of the order are enclosed within the papers and handed to *privates* or Non-commiss[ioned] officers. In this way, Thousands of copies are passed inside of the enemy's lines every day.

There is no picket fighting now. In fact, the armys are on quite intimate terms. When they [meet] the first thing is to shake hands, then a chew of tobacco, then sit down and chat. The parting is that of old friends—a hearty shake of hand, many wishes of good "luck," a Good by, and they walk in sepperate directions, mutually pleased with each other. Thus it is to day. Tomorrow both armys may be transformed into Demons, each recklessly striving to annihilate the other. In talking with a prisoner taken on Sunday morning, [I] wanted to know what he thought of the yankees! We don't call "yons *yankees*—you are North Western troops." Some who had been in the great Eastern battles said they never saw fighting before. Another remarked "youns" fight moore like devils than men.

Yesterday Gen. Critenden paid his Farewell vis[i]ts to the different regiments of the old 21st army corps.[4] He called on Col. Aldrich, complimented the "old 44th," [and] talked over old times when it was in his *Div.* [He] said there was never a better regiment engaged. We all feel that in him we have lost a true and noble Soldier, a warm-harted friend, and a perfect Gentleman. Later was over to 14th O[hio]. Saw Chris Graves[5] and I. Donat. The ballance of my acquaintens are among the "killed, wounded, and missing." We now draw full rations of meat and bread, half rations of coffe and sugar, with no vegetabls. We have all we really need to eat. Last night I *dreamed* that you had received the money I sent Three months since, which is all I *have heard* of it. Will you please inform me whether you received it or not? Seventy dollars is rather moore than I care about loosing if it can be avoided. O! Yes—how would you like the idea of my enlisting in the "Iron Brigade?" You know they offer $400.00 Bounty. I can tell you what I think about it—that is that *money* won't hire me to reenlist.[6] But I must close. One of our boys leaves for the "United Stats" tomorrow. So good by. Heaven bless and keep you from harm is the constant p[r]ayer of *yourn own*

George

Awful lonly. No letters.

1. After Chickamauga, the Federal government rushed reinforcements to the Army of the Cumberland that had hunkered down in Chattanooga. Maj. Gen. Joseph Hooker came from Virginia with the XI Corps under Maj. Gen. Oliver O. Howard and the XII Corps under Maj. Gen. Henry W. Slocum. Maj. Gen. Franz Sigel had commanded the XI Corps from September 1862 to February 1863. He did not come to the West with his old command. Maj. Gen. William T. Sherman brought elements of the XV and XVI Corps from Grant's army in the Mississippi Valley. Grant took command of all Federal forces in the Chattanooga area.

2. The XX and XXI Corps were consolidated to form the new IV Corps. When all the changes were completed, the 44th Indiana was part of the 3d Brigade, 3d Division, IV Corps. Brig. Gen. Samuel Beatty commanded the brigade.

   In the reorganization, Aldrich was appointed provost marshal of Chattanooga, and the 44th Indiana, commanded by Maj. (later Lt. Col.) Joseph C. Hodges, became part of the city's garrison. Although no one knew it at the time, this new assignment meant that the regiment would participate in no more great battles.

3. Strong rivalries existed between troops who had been fighting in the West and those sent from Virginia to their assistance. The report of about six hundred Confederates having been killed was false.

4. Relieved of his command in the West on October 9, 1863, Crittenden was transferred to the East, where he took command of a division in the IX Corps.

5. Probably Christian R. Graves, who enlisted in Company G, 14th Ohio, on August 26, 1861, for three years. He was promoted to corporal December 15, 1863, and to sergeant December 17, 1864. He was mustered out with the company July 11, 1865. *Ohio Roster,* vol. 2, 438.

6. This was a generic term used to refer to soldiers who had extended their terms of service ("veteranized," in army jargon) and accepted the bounty for having done so. Squier probably did not intend to refer to the "Iron Brigade," a unit that served in the Union army in Virginia. He may have meant the expression as a reference to his own regiment, commonly known as the "Iron 44th."

LETTER 19

Chattanooga, Tenn. Oct. 17th, '63

Very Dear Ellen,

I don't know that there is much for me to write from the fact I don't feel *inspierd.* Yours mailed 1st inst. is received. In regard to the land, I have already answered you.

Besides, I rather wish to hear further from you before giving my final answer. By the by, the great excitment in camp now is Gov. Morton's proposition to the war department to recall one of the oldest or most depleted regiments of each Congressional district to go into camp in their respective districts until recruited to its max., which is one thousand and ten men, *Provided* that two thirds of the regiment (now in the field) will reenlist for three years from the present time or during the war. In case the proposition be accepted, the regt. such as reenlist will be mustered out, paid up all dues including the $100.00 bounty, and will be entitled to the $400.00 offered to "veterans." Those who do not reenlist will be attached to some other regiment and serve the ballance of the term of their enlistment. Now the question is whether to reenlist or *not*. I'm sure I hardly know whether it is my duty to continue in the service while there are so many at home who have not done their part, nor will they unless <co>mpeled to. Now Ellen, I would really like you to give your opinion. You will won't you?[1]

All is quiet along the line. The enemy is repo[r]ted one hundred and Seventy five thousand strong in front but that is doubtless exagerated.[2] O! Yes, I came near forgetting to tell you that you need not send the gloves, as I had an opportunity of buying qu[i]te cheap, $1.00, and so am supplied. Write often will you, to your loving

George

1. As 1864 approached, the Federal government faced the possibility of losing the regiments that had entered service in 1861 for three years. At the very least, the discharge of such competent, veteran troops would have weakened the national armies and prolonged the war. To avoid the loss of the old troops, the government instituted a series of measures to encourage the men to reenlist. These inducements included monetary bounties, a thirty-day furlough, and the privilege of designating themselves as "veteran volunteers." Most of the veteran regiments, like the 44th Indiana, remained in the service. For comments on "veteranizing" in the 44th Indiana, see Rerick, *The Forty-fourth Indiana Volunteer Infantry*, 106–8.

2. Although some Federals accepted very high estimates of Rebel strength (see *OR*, vol. 30, pt. 1, 233), most—like Squier—did not. Bragg's army numbered about sixty-six thousand.

Chapter 3. 1864

ᗉ

LETTER 1

Chattanooga May 26, 1864

My Own Darling,

Your very welcome letter of 14th Inst. is just received and I was so glad to know that you was well and that Ella's eyes were better. O what would I not give to see again entirely well that dear good creature. How I have pittied her when she used to stay in that dark and dreary room alone, day after day, week after week. You know what my fears were at one time—that she would go entirely blind. How perfectly awful— how much worse than death would it have been. Now that she is really getting bet- ter how ve[r]y thankful ought we to feel. Even now there [is] a feeling of uncertainty, of dread that she may yet loose her sight. Perhaps I have not sufficient confidence in the future. If so, it has been occasioned by repeated disappointments, from a *knowl- edge* of the uncertainty of all things. I am not among the number that think all hu- man happiness is visionary, that there is *no Earthly* happiness. On the contrary, I *know* that there is real, true, *solid* enjoyment if we will but accept it at our Father's hand. Love—the foundation of our religion, of all good, the ruleing Atribute of the Great and Mighty Ruler of the Universe—is happiness complete. "This world's *not* all a fleeting show for man's illusion given."[1]

Later in the day. My health is very good, though last night I had to suffer the pen- alty of intemperance. I did not feel very well last evening. At supper time we had some very fine tomato pickles, of which I partook rather freely. In the night I woke up and felt O! How sick. Got up, "disgorged," went back to bed and slept well the ballance of the night. This morning am all right. You must not feel jealous of Charlote be- cause I sent her my Photo before I sent one to you. The reason was it was a very poor picture and I wanted to get a better one for *you*. You know if there is any *best* you should have it. I have sat again. The Prints will be out the first of next week, when I shal send you my *Phiz* [physiognomy] in as good order as it can be taken at this place. But it is impossible to get a fine picture here. In the first place, instead of having a nicely furnished Gallery, they have but a ammo tent. Then they often get out of necessary chemicals. I have a small Album, nearly full, of Photos of our Co. which I shal send home in a short time. The Album you will accept; the pictures you will doubtless not for but which I think a great deal of. Most of them are men with whom I have associated for the past three years, with whom I have passed th[r]ough many dangers and togeth[er] endured many hardships and privations. So perhaps it is not strange that I should feel differently about them than others.

After dress parade. It is allmost dark, and I am [on] duty tomorrow so I must close this to night, for it certainly would not do to let your letter [go] two whole days unanswered. The weather for a day or two past has been delightfully and pleasant with occasional Showers of rain—real mountain thunder Showers.

Candle light. As to the papers, you need [not] send them at present, as we get plenty of religious reading through the Christian commission.[2] If we should be sent to [the] f[r]ont or any other place where we were not supplied through that channel, the "Record" would be very acceptable and I would let you know. The last three weeks has certainly seemed as long to me as it *could* to you. I cannot realize that has been less than three weeks since we parted on that dismal morning.[3] It certainly seems an age. I think it will not be best for Wilber to work out much. He surely will have work enough to do at home. He is not very "stout" you know and I do not want him to overdo and permanently injure his health and make him old while he is yet young.

Enclosed you will find $40 Greenback, which you will use as you please. If you have the money to spare I would like to have you pay Father what we owe him, as I do not wish to commence liveing off of the farm. I drew $150. Had some things I had to get. Owed Saml. Hartle[4] $20, which made rather a large hole in the odd 50. I have now just $20 left, which I think may answer until another pay day. If it does not, I shal have to borrow, for now I cannot live without money. Every thing we eat has to be paid for down. My eyes are rather week, so I must close for this time. Give my love to all the friends. Tell Wilber that I should like to have him write. A kiss for our little darlings and right here ——— I send one to *my darling*. Good night. Heaven bless and keep you all and hasten the time when I shal again be permitted to see those loving faces is the prayer of your ever loving
Husband

If Mrs. Hartle[5] and Mr. Palmer's[6] fo[l]ks make up a box and it perfectly you may send me a little (or much) dried fruit.
George

It is rather extravagant to leave so much blank paper but I ha[r]dly know how to a[v]oid [it] this time. Good by my darling.

Will you please send Aunt Solomes's[7] address?

1. Squier apparently purposely misquoted Thomas Moore's "This World Is All a Fleeting Show." Moore's text began: "This world is all a fleeting show, For man's illusion given." See *A Library of Poetical Literature in Thirty-Two Volumes* (New York, 1902), vol. 1, 226.
2. The Christian Commission was a civilian organization that distributed religious publications to Union soldiers.

3. The regiment was in Indiana on veteran furlough in February and early March (see Letter 19, note 1 in chapter 2). It is unknown why Squier was there in early May.

4. Samuel Hartel from Hall's Corners was mustered in March 3, 1864. He was killed at Chattanooga on July 13, 1864.

5. Mrs. Hartle is unidentified except by context. She possibly was related to the Hartle (Hartel) mentioned above.

6. Palmer may have been Pvt. Lucius C. Palmer of Hall's Corners, who was mustered in January 27, 1864, and served with the company until mustered out September 14, 1865, as a corporal.

7. Aunt Solomes is unidentified except by context.

LETTER 2

[No place, September 1864]

Though you may think I place undue weight on the result of the comeing election, yet I am sincere when I say that so sure as the sun shines at noon day, might the success of the democracy be considered the death nell of our Republic. Perhaps you may think me severe on the great Genl. McClellan.[1] You may ask what he has said or done to warrant my conclusions. *A man is known by the company he keeps,* and you well know that every *copperhead, peace snake, and outspoken rebel* of the North will sustain and vote for the democratic candidate for the Presidency. The man who associates with and stands side by side to such men as Fernand[o] Wood, Valandigham, Cox, Vorhus and the like is in my opinion competent to perform any act however despisable, traitorous, or dishonorable.[2] Had I engaged to furnish his Satanic majesty with a thousand souls for perdition, I would tender him *one* such as the above and claim that I had filled the contract. Last night I *did* think I would let politics alone for to night, but you know out of the abundance of the heart the mouth speaketh, and the same is true with writing. Besides, you requested me (if I mistake not) to write just what was in my mind, so if I should rather bore you by harping [on] one subject you must submit with as good grace as possable. I have sometimes almost come to the conclusion that you have a one idea man for your husband. Don't mind thinking so myself, but would not like to force you to that conclusion by my stile of writing. You need have no fears for my health, as it is much better now than for months past, and doubtless will continue to improove as I am having such an easy time. But my eyelids are getting rather heavy and my head *kinder mixed up* so I will wind up for to night. The fact is I must surely try and get moore sleep than I have for some time past, as I think that I hardly sleep enough for health. It is now 11 o'clock. The wind [is] blowing a perfect storm; a heavy shower is comeing up from the N.W., and I will say good night.

4th. Many cowardly hearts beat low to night in fear of the result of tomorrow's day's work.[3] Many traitorous scoundrels will turn uneasily in their beds, resolving in their mind their chances of being forced to take up arms against their erring brethren, of being forced by the "despotic government" to fight against their friends. It is really to[o] bad that they should be compeled to fight against the men and principals and institutions which they worship, and all this by an abolitionist, by the despot who now rules this nation. Poor fellows, I feel sorry for them in [?]. If I could have my way, every man subject to military duty in the Northern states would have a musket placed in their hands in less than thirty days, and I would not deal very gently with them either. [I] would like to command a company of those conscripts. It would do me good to bring the cowardly snakes to time to show them the beauties of soldiering.

Don Bowers was here this evening. His regt. [the] 18th Mich. is on their way home, having served three years. The 30 Ind. is also on their way home, that is the non vet. part of it.[4] When I see men of my acqaintance homeward bound, it is with dificulty that I keep from getting in a perfect panic to go to[o], but I think of the maxim "let thy fair *wisdom* not thy *passion* sway."[5] I feel now moore as though we were contending for something real, something tangable than ever before, and were it not for my bad health, am not sure but that I should consider it my duty to stay in the service until the great object was attained. For surely one's obligations does not cease as long as the necessity exists, and the government surely has a claim on every able bodied loyal man until the great end is attained, the mighty work accomplished, and the redemption of the enthralled complete, and we become not only in name but in *reality* a free people, and we can consistently claim that America ofers an asylum for the opressed of *all nations,* not excluding even Africa, until even the despised negro can find safety and liberty under [the] broad folds of the American baner. Well, I must stop, for I will send moore than two of these sheets in one letter.

When I commenced writing this evening I had no intention of doing moore than finishing up that sheet. But as it is not my bed time yet, of cou[rse] there is nothing for me to do but commence on this, though I really am at something at a loss for something to [write] about which may interest you. But then, I remember you told me that *anything* I happened to be thinking about would interest you. Shal I tell you why I would prefer Mr. Lincoln for President of the United State[s] for the next four years before any other man? In the first place, he has the experience which no other man in this nation has. He is entirely devoted to the *true* interests of the Government. He is a *man* [who] *thinks and acts for himself.* And last but not least, *he is a Christian.* The *republican* Government can[not] endure except it be founded on the pure principals of the Bible, and we must have not only statesmen but we must have *Christian* rulers. The Bible out of which rise the forms as well as the spirit of free institutions enjoins this policy on the part of the people: "The God of Iseral [Israel] said, the rock of Iseral spake unto me: He that ruleth over men must be just, ruling in the fear of God," and in another place that they should pro[v]ide for their rulers able men such as fear God.[6] They wer[e] to hate covetousness, and they were to be men of truth. The influence of the administration of such rulers upon national virtue, prosperity, and true greatness is described in many places as "He shal be as the light of the morning when the sun riseth without clouds" and "as showers of rain

upon the earth," &c.[7] Then is not the true theory of national prosperity and greatness clearly unfolded in the revealed word of God? And is not the secret of all stability and human greatness in the governments of earth found alone in the purifying
influence of Christianity? This alone, pervading the mind and body politic, can make
a true and lasting republic.

My eyes have been rather weak for several days and now they admonish me that I
must stop using them whether I am sleepy or not. But when I get to writing with no
one around to disturb, it is the easiest matter in the world to spin out a great long
letter, and after it is done perhaps may not contain one single new idea which will
be of use to any living creature. But then it certainly is a pleasure for me [to] write to
you just what happens to come into my mind, and I have your word (which is satisfactory to me) that it is a pl[e]asure for you [to] read whatever I happen to write. So,
according to that it is without doubt the most profitable way for me to "kill time."
But I *must* stop for to night.

Monday evening or rather night. I had intended filling this sheet, but had company this evening. A Lt. of 79 Ind., one of my old army friends, spent the evening
quite pleasantly. Well, I suppose there is but little doubt but that we go home to vote
to day. We were required to furnish a list of the votes of the company and regiment.
In our Co. there is thirty four, all of which will vote for Lincoln and Morton.[8] We
have just learned that the draft has been indefinately postponed. I doubt the policy,
for it seems to me very necessary that we have moore men imediately, for without
another great victory I fear the result of the presidential election.[9] If Richmond *could*
be taken, Lincoln's reelection would be a moral certainty. It is not late but for some
reason I am sleepy, and as this must go out tomorrow morning or it may not reach
you next Thursday week I will close. So good night. Remember me to the friends,
and when I say friends I include Mr. and Mrs. Murphy[10] and various others to[o]
numerous to mention. Once moore good night.

G.W. Squier

1. Maj. Gen. George B. McClellan had commanded the principal Union army in Virginia
   1861–62. While he had never enjoyed success, McClellan suffered no great defeats either.
   His disputes with the Republicans in general, and with the Lincoln administration in
   particular, made him a hero to the Democrats. They chose him as their presidential candidate in 1864. While McClellan and most Northern Democrats favored a conservative
   war waged only for the purpose of preserving the Union, by 1864 Lincoln and the Republicans had embraced the abolition of slavery as an essential war aim.
2. These men were all leading critics of the North's war policy. Fernando Wood, a former
   mayor of New York City, once threatened to have that metropolis declare itself an inde-
   pendent city. He was an antiwar member of Congress 1863–65. By 1864, Clement L.
   Vallandigham had become the most prominent critic of the war in the North. He ran
   unsuccessfully for governor of Ohio in 1863 and played an important role in Democratic
   party affairs in 1864. Samuel Sullivan Cox was a Democratic representative from Ohio

and a staunch McClellan supporter. He favored a negotiated settlement with the South and opposed turning the war into a crusade against slavery. Daniel Vorhees was a Democratic senator from Illinois and a bitter critic of Federal war policies.

3. A reference to the draft to be held on September 5.

4. The name Bowers (or similar spellings) does not appear in the roster of the 18th Michigan.

5. See Shakespeare, *Twelfth Night,* act 4, scene 1, line 56.

6. See 2 Sam. 23:3 and Exod. 18:21.

7. See 2 Sam. 23:4. The latter quotation could, in fact, be Squier's attempt to reproduce any of several biblical passages, including 2 Samuel 23:3, Psalm 72:6, and Job 38:26.

8. Republican politicians, fearful of losing the approaching election, wanted to send home as many Hoosier soldiers as possible to vote. (Indiana did not permit its soldiers to vote in the field.) Some nine thousand voting-age Indiana soldiers from rear-echelon units like the 44th Indiana, or men who were disabled from field duty, were sent home to vote. One officer of the 44th Indiana made it home just an hour before the polls closed (Rerick, *The Forty-fourth Indiana Volunteer Infantry,* 113). Like those men in Squier's company, they voted overwhelmingly for Republican candidates. As it turned out, however, the soldier votes only added to the Republicans' margin of victory. The troops who captured Atlanta in early September contributed far more to the Republicans' triumphs in October and November than did the men sent home to vote. See David E. Long, *The Jewel of Liberty: Abraham Lincoln's Re-election and the End of Slavery* (Mechanicsburg, Pa., 1994), especially ch. 12.

9. Although under tremendous pressure from his fellow Republicans to postpone the draft until after the election, Lincoln refused to do so. See Long, *Jewel of Liberty,* 221–22.

10. The Murphys are unidentified except by context.

LETTER 3

Chattanooga, Tenn. Sept. 8th, 1864

My Darling,

It seems an age since the rct. of your last dear good loving letter. But what is worse, there appears little prospects of hearing from you for some time to come. Wheeler is ruining the road from here to Nashville and the consequence is no letters, no Northern papers, nor anything else, and it seems so lonely that I can scarcely endure it.[1] Is it not to[o] bad that we should be shut out from the rest of the world just now as the draft is comeing off and expectation of stirring news from Grant?[2] Of course, there is but one thing for us to do, which is simply to wait the good pleasure of our erring brother and his band of marauders, horse thieves, and murderers. I was talking with a Government employee from Lagrange Co., Indiana who was captured and paroled while at work some fifteen miles up the river from this place. There was about fifty men in all. Among them was three negroes which was taken out, placed in a row, and shot down dead. This was done for no prov[oc]ation whatever—only that they were negroes and hired for wages to the Government. He who thinks such atrocities

can be committed with impunity, without calling down the vengence of Heaven, is
doomed to disappointment. But I will stop, for I see I'm getting on the old subject
of the nigger.[3]

Egypt had its plagues and its all-consuming swarms of locusts. Beautiful tropical
regions are cursed with the deadly upas tree. Delig[h]tful valleys are swept with
distructive floods. But the United States are afflicted with a curse worse than all
these—treason—secession. The displeasure of the Deity stamps itself on all things
animate or inanimate that are touched by the acursed principal of treason. Secession
is death—distruction—ruin—everything good and pure and holy is blasted and
blackened by contact with it. Virtue gives place to the most degrading vice. Honor
and chastity become obsolete and are to be considered only as things that were.
Oppression, grief, and want produce their legitimate results, and the comon people
become recklessly indifferent to the welfare of either body or soul. Society is become
a moral charnal house, a loathsome stagnant pool. And yet there is a great party at
the north calling itself *"Democricy"* that meets in convention in a great city in the
free state to nominate candidates for the highest office within the gift of the people,
and utters no word of condemnation or censure against the mighty evils embodied
in this one hateful word *secession*. They cry mightily with a loud voice *peace* and hug
the vile, detested monster closely to their bosoms.[4] Just as our nation has passed the
crisis of war, just as victory is perching upon our banner,[5] they ask us to cease the
application of the successful remedy and try the benign influence of moral suasion,
of compromise. What do these gentlemen wish? What will they have? They would
substitute popguns for cannon. Sugar-coated pills man[u]factured of compromise and
armistice are prescribed in the place of Minnie balls.[6] The era of sedatives and ano-
dynes is to begin, and the millennium is then surely to begin. The monster secession
is caressed and patted on the back, called a good fellow, and invited to come and reign
over us, fixing its own conditions. We are to wear sackcloth, crawl [on] our bellys,
and eat dirt as penance for our sins in rebelling against the authority elect of the south,
who in times past controled the "democracy" and ministered to them in things politic.[7] The "common heritage" is then to be divided up, but our dear southern brethren are to have the first choice, which is to be duly delivered up without demur or
even debate. This is to be the great *general* principal on which peace is to be restored.
Then comes in "collateral questions" which can easily be adjusted. Of course, we shal
be ready to deliver into the fair hands of our erring brethren all the *chattles* that have
seceeded from their master, as well as those who may secede in the near or far off
future.[8] This is what the great democratic party would do. It is what they have declared to the world, but moore especially, to their poor oppressed brethren of the
southern confederacy. They would have peace on any terms, howsoever dishonorable to the nation, howsoever degrading to the northern people. Having killed or
crippled two thirds of the traitorous scoundrels of the south, the peace-loving democracy would require us to deify what remains. And having also by untold hardships and privations and at the cost of hundreds of thousan[d]s of lives conquered
and reclaimed two thirds of the territory once subject to secession, we are now to

give it all back without complaint, and on our bended knees pray for the forgiveness of our sins in thus trampling upon the rights of our worthy lords and superiors. Never, *never*, so long as life remains, as there is a God in Heaven, will we now submit to this base, cowardly concession. The soil of a thousand battlefields is sprinkled with the blood of martyrs to the union. That soil is sacred—moore, it is doubly sacred and has been consecrated to liberty and union forever, and no vile secessionist shal polute it with his acursed foot and live, or whisper his detested creed of treason to the breezes that are wafted over the bones of those dead heroes and go unpunished. The submissionist[s] at Chicago are mistaken in the spirit of the army if they suppose they will submit to the vile principals there promulgated. Submission is for the week and erring, for those whose cowardly hearts would accept any terms so that safety was secured, and not for the strong and virtuous. The one party may deem it honorable, or at least prudent. The other can only look upon it as odious in the extreme, and not to be thought of—what acknow[l]edges to our enemies and to the whole world what we know to be false—that for the last three years we have been waging a war of oppression? A war simply of conquest? Admit that it is no great principal for which we are contending? "Forbid it Almighty God." And yet we know if the democratic party gets in power, it will be done. They are pledged body and soul to the southern confederacy, and only want the power and our enemys and their friends [to] have it all their own way. But I do not fear; I feel sure that right and justice in its broadest sence will succeed, and that the great sacrifice allready made and yet to be made will not be in vain. I think we will come out of this prepared for the great destiny for which this nation was designed.[9]

Well, I will stop right here. But I must congratulate you that you[r] somwhat of a l[e]n[g]thy epistle to read from your abolition husband without the "nigger" in once I believe, but am not certain. Of one thing I am certain: that it is not *all* nigger and abolitionism. So you see that I'm not allways thinking on one subject. Perhaps it was not strange that I felt like writing somewhat extensively on that matter, as I [k]new perfectly well how you felt about it, and I certainly wanted to tell *all* that I felt on the subject befor I could rest easy. The fit is off now, so you will doubtless enjoy a little rest.

O! Yes, Sam Hartle[10] expects to start home in a day or two. Will doubtless get there before you receive [this]. Trains have again commenced running to Nashville, so tomorrow I expect a letter. It seems an age since the rct. of your last short one. Don't imagine I feel like complaining at the shortness (that's an elegant expression is[n]'t it) of your letters (though I do love long ones). I am to[o] thankful for your promptness in writing every week. How in the world should I live if you wrote no oftener than the majority of women do to their husbands in the army—say, once in about three or four weeks? The fact is, I should die *sure* or resign imediately or enlist for during life or something else very desperate indeed.

The rainy season is comeing on and I wish I had profited by your suggestion and sent up my papers some time ago. Now I might have been ready to start home, but now must bide my time, or rather the time of the return of the regiment.[11] It's rain-

ing and is about bed time, so I might as well close. I did calculate to fill this sheet
this evening, but after changing the subject on which I commen[ced] writing matter soon run out. The fact is I'm a miserable hand, or what would be nearer the truth,
have a miserable head for writing, especially common place, every[day] things such
as one expects and perhaps desires. But "there's no use talking." I *can't* write a letter
of tolerable length, especially while laying in camp with nothing of interest
transpireing, nothing to discribe, nothing but every day life—dull, dreary, and entirely devoid [of] interest to myself and others. The only way for me to produce a
letter even of tollerable length under thes circumstances is to take up some subject
on which I feel interested and let the mind run. That method has its objections. In
the first place, the matter may not meet the aprobation of the reader. If it should,
then the m[a]nner may fail to interest. And last but not least, there appears to be no
stopping point. This last may be obviated by never sitting down to write until nearly
bed time. For the others, there appears to be no remedy. I will stop right here, so good
night Ellen. Heaven bless and preserv you all. Remember me as ever your own
loving husband

G.W. Squiers

When I stopped writing Sundy evening I enclosed and mailed, expecting to send
it out next morning, but there has been no trains running North yet. But [they] will
doubtless to day, as the morning paper announces seven days mail to be distributed
this morning. You can hardly imagine what a hurry I'm in for it to come around, for
there will be one letter for me sure and perhaps moore. The work for the commission will be closed up this week when the institution will doubtless be broken up.
Then whether the regiment gets back or not, I shal try and get my papers started,
though it is quite uncertain whe[the]r they will come back approved by the higher
authorities without first hav[in]g the approoval of the regimental officers. But certainly canot know until I try, and the fact is I am getting in an awful fever to leave
this wilderness of war and again for a season at least enjoy the society of the loved
ones at home. It has rained almost incessently for the last week. The camp is not
muddy but the blankets and clothing are damp and smell disagreeably. The fact is
one can scarcely keep from getting *very blue,* especially when they are the least bit in
[a] word homesick, which I think may be [the] case with me. Hoping that I shal not
long have to continue this method of communication with you, I am again as ever
your own

George

1. In August, in an effort to force the Union army in Georgia to retreat, the Confederates
   sent Wheeler's cavalry to wreck the rail lines that supplied the invading Yankees. Although,
   as Squier relates, the raiders did some damage, the effect was not serious enough to compel
   the Federals to abandon their campaign in Georgia. Indeed, a week before this letter was

written, the Rebels had been forced to evacuate Atlanta because the Federals had managed to cut the railroads that supplied the city.

2. In July the Federal government had called for five hundred thousand more volunteers. If that number did not come forth by September 5, Lincoln would draft as many men as necessary to raise the new troops. Grant, although commanding all Union armies, had taken personal command of operations in Virginia. In September 1864 his army remained, as it had remained for months, bogged down before the massive Rebel fortifications at Richmond and Petersburg.

3. Federals frequently alleged that the Confederates murdered captured blacks who were in the military service of the United States. Many of these accusations were valid. No details are known of the specific instance to which Squier refers.

4. At its convention in Chicago, the Democratic Party had adopted a platform pronouncing the war a failure and calling for a negotiated settlement. Implementation of such a proposal would have meant Confederate independence.

5. This refers to the capture of Atlanta that resulted in ensuring the defeat of the Democrats in the fall elections.

6. Minié balls were deadly lead conoidal projectiles widely used during the war.

7. In the immediate antebellum decades, many Northerners resented the control the South allegedly held over the Democratic Party and, through that party, over the Federal government. Often the South used that power to block legislation desired by Northerners. See the comments in Letter 5.

8. The reference is to slaves who had escaped from their masters and reached Union-controlled territory. See Squier's comments in Letter 4.

9. Compare the words and thoughts expressed here with the text of Lincoln's Gettysburg Address.

10. Squier obviously is confused here. Samuel Hartel was killed at Chattanooga on July 13, 1864. Samuel Hartle, listed by Dr. Rerick as "unassigned," was "unaccounted for" after March 3, 1864. See Rerick, *The Forty-fourth Indiana Volunteer Infantry*, 170, 212.

11. Although the regiment was part of the Chattanooga garrison, it had been sent to middle Tennessee in August to help defend the area against Confederate cavalry. It returned to Chattanooga on September 14 but left again on the twenty-seventh. See John T. Lane to Brother and Sister, October 11, 1864, 44th Indiana file, Longstreet-Thomas Library, Chickamauga-Chattanooga National Military Park. (The editors thank Jim Ogden for making this document available to them.)

Squier then was serving on a military commission in Chattanooga and, therefore, did not accompany the unit. See the postscript to this letter and Letters 4, 5, and 7.

LETTER 4

Chatta., Tenn. Sept. 28, '64

Darling,

I'm lonely to night—depressed—sad—and perhaps not without cause, for a telegram received this eveni[n]g announces the death of Col. Hodges[1] of our regiment. Yesterday morning at 4 o'clock orders were received for the regiment to prepare to leave imediately with three days rations. At 7 they marched down to the depot, took the train, and started north as was supposed to assist Gen. Reausea[2] to drive Forest[3] and Wheeler from our lines. And this evening as I said a telegram dated at Tallahoma on the N. C. R. R. [Nashville–Chattanooga Railroad] was rcd. stating that last night Col. Hodges was run over by the train and killed. He came out with the regt. as 1st. Lt. and by his soldierly conduct had worked his way up [to] the highest position in the regt. Though he fell not where he could have wished to fall—at the head of his column, cheering and sustaining it against the enemy—yet he has sealed his faith with his blood. He has offered up his life on the alter of his country. He has left a record of which his friends may not feel ashamed. His life for the past three years is inseperably connected with the history of this regt., and is it saying to[o] much to say that the record of the 44th Indiana regiment is full of patriotic devotion and soldierly virtues? Its casualties on many bloody fields have left "aching voids" at many firesides—"bravely it fought and well"[4] at Donnoldson, Shiloh, Corinth, Lavergne, Stoneriver, and Chickamauga. And in all these in different capacities has J.C. Hodges, our late commander, bourne a prominent part. He is gone—never moore shal we see his smileing face, never moore shal we hear his clear voice ringing out in commands to "his boys." Is it not sad that one so young and so much beloved by all who knew him should thus be called from among us—he so full of life and hope, with prospects fair for long life and happiness and competent of doing a great deal of good in the world. But he fell in one of the most glorious of causes that ever engaged the attention of mankind since the world began. I think it is Bates or Cupper or some of our poets who says in speaking of this war and those who fall in defe[ense] of the right.

> The blood that flows for freedom is God's blood;
> Who dies for man's redemption dies with Christ;
> The plan of expiation is unchanged
> And as one died supremely good for all
> So one dies still that many moore may live . . .
> So fall our saviours on the bloody field
> And with their blood they wash the nation clean
> And furnish expiation for the sin
> That those who slay them have been guilty of . . .
> This is God's plan—the changeless plan of Heaven
> The good die that the evil may be purged
> The noble perish that the base may live
> The free are bound that slaves may break their bonds
> Those who have happy homes are self-exiled
> That other exiles may have happy homes
> The harvest sons of Freedom's land are slain

That the oppressed of tyrant's realms may live
The guilty land is washed in innocent blood
And Slavery is thus atoned for by the free.[5]

Then why weep for the departed? Why mourn for the slain? Why be cast down for the loss of one whom God deems worthy for the sacrifice that shall redeem a nation from her sins and blot out the blackest spot that ever darkened the escutcheon of any nation? Why think that any sacrifice, however great, is to[o] much to be offered upon the alter of liberty? Why think that any price is to[o] great for freedom! Not of the few only but of *all*, whatsoever their color or caste. For sure it is that slavery has no foundation in the moral stability of justice. It is lighted by no beam from heaven— it is blessed by no prayer of man—it is worshiped with no gratitude by the patriot. It has remained among us. Its appointed time, its hour has come, and the whole earth resounds with its fall. And the same sun which has measured out with reluctance its impious life will soon pour its undecaying beams amid its ruins and bring forth from the earth which it has overshadowed the bright flowers of spring, the delicious fruit of liberty. Instead of a nation of slaves, it will be a band of freemen. Why will men talk of compromise now that we are so near the goal of our wishes? Why talk of an armistice now that the monster is in his death struggle? Has not three years of desperate resistan[ce] to the nation's authority, three years of war with its lessons of bitterness and grief and death and agony worse than death convinced us that compromise is *impossable* even if desireable? My eyes admonish me that I have used them long enough so I *must* quit, though don't like to. Good night.

30th. I am lonely to night—the boys all gone, no northern papers, and of course no letters. The last train from Nashville came in last Sunday morning and this is Friday night—allmost a week. And what is discour[aging] is that there is no prospect of mail for some time to come. The enemy, twenty-five thousand strong, is in our rear on an electioneering tour for the democratic nominee. Hope he will have a pleasant time *in a home.* Genl. Thomas with the old 4th Corps in town and leave[s] for the north to night, doubtless to pay their compliments to Forest, Wheeler & Co., agents of "Little Mac."[6]

Well, there is now no hopes of the Indiana soldiers going home, so as soon as the regiment comes back I shal send up my papers. Would do so imediately, but they have to be approved by the regt. officers. Have not drawn my pay yet—am out of money and have to live with the boys (there is three which did not go with the company). Of course it is not expensive, but I don't like the idea of spunging. But under the circumstances, it is the only alternative. Have been half sick all day and don't feel like writing to night. And as there is [not] probability of sending this out for several days to come, it will not pay to make an effort.

Oct. 2nd. It is Sunday and yet no mail from the north. How very lonely and how difficult to keep from having the blues just a little. While thinking of our "trials and tribulations" the mind naturly coms back to the *cause* which is secession. And as I have nothing to do, I will examine this subject of secession and see if there be any element of good, any redeeming quality beneath its odious exterior (I don't expect to write anything to be of use, only to kill time and keep off the blues). It is a creation conceived of sin, born of iniquity, and nursed and reared by the mischievous dogma of States Rights as inculcated in the south—the right to sacrifice the many for the few, the right to destroy a whole comunity to gratify the ambition of a single individual, the right to tear down a "temple of beauty in order to erect a pigsty upon the ruins." Admit this doctrine of State Rights or what is the same, the right of secession, and our whole social and political edifice falls to the ground. First, States secede from the union by simply resolving themselves out. Then the people, becoming inoculated with the deadly virus, discard the political doctrines and traditions of the Fathers, renounce the right of men to govern, declare as arbitrary all law and order for the regulation of society, and ignore the fellowship of men born in other latitude[s], with other thoughts and habits of life. Nor will it stop here. Husbands secede from their wives, sons and brothers from the fraternal hearthstone, *error* unconfined escapes from its subordination to truth and sets up for itself, and anarchy stands ready to step in and complete the ruin. There is one and but one redeeming fact in the whole catalogue of consequences of secession, which is that the negro secedes from his master, and ceasing to be the property of another, he declares to the world that he is a *man,* and ready and anxious to act his part as such in the great drama of life. [He] announces the fact that henceforth he takes upon himself self ownership, which is God's best gift to man and guara[n]teed by the Declaration of Independence. If I am not careful I shal get on to the "nigger question." If you could look about me here in this war cursed city, once so beautiful and teaming with life and wealth and ease, you would see *secession* written all over its shattered buildings—its deserted homes—its decayed flower gardens—its gravel walks overgrown with weeds and its mansions once elegant but now fast going to decay. You enter the grounds of what was once a superior home and stroll about among deserted pathways plan[n]ed by tast[e] and executed with elegance and once frequented perhaps by doting parents and happy children, and your heart sickens with the thoughts that force themselves upon you. You feel like one who "treads slow" amid the ruins and landmarks of domestic happiness, the light of which has gone out and left only the dismal picture of what once existed. You will listen for the "patter of little feet" and the hum of merry voices, but you hear them not. Marks of desolation are around you, and silence reigns supreme. Crime and treason to a benificent government have made outcasts of parents and children, and sent them away before the advent of the *"Lincoln hirelings," "the relentless invaders."* "God shal punish the wicked." He is now punishing them, nor will that punishment cease until they repent of their sins and turn from their evil ways. What can there be moore wicked than secession? The Angel that seceded was hurled from the battlements of Heaven. Our good old grandmother seceded from the government of God and was driven from that beautiful posy garden. Sodom and Gommora seceded from the govern[ment] of high Heaven and they likewise were punished for their secession.

1. Lt. Col. Joseph C. Hodges of Elkhart entered service with the regiment on September 20, 1861, as a first lieutenant in Company I. He became regimental adjutant on November 22, 1861, was promoted to major on October 24, 1863, and to lieutenant colonel on July 27, 1864. The railroad accident in which he was mortally injured occurred near Tullahoma, Tennessee, when he fell between two moving cars. One of his legs and the other foot were cut off. He died soon afterward. He was never a colonel.
2. Maj. Gen. Lovell H. Rousseau commanded the District of Nashville.
3. Maj. Gen. (later Lt. Gen.) Nathan Bedford Forrest, who commanded Confederate cavalry in Mississippi, was then raiding in west-central Tennessee.
4. A brief and modified quotation (changed to the singular) from Tennyson's "Charge of the Light Brigade."
5. The editors have been unable to verify the poet or source of this quotation.
6. "Little Mac"—Maj. Gen. George B. McClellan, whose chances of winning the election would be greatly enhanced by a significant Confederate victory—was the Democratic nominee for president in November 1864. Maj. Gen. George H. Thomas was sent to Tennessee from the Federal army in Georgia along with the IV Corps and other troops to defend Tennessee from the Confederates.

LETTER 5

Chattanooga Oct. 5th, 1864

Dear Ellen,

Last night I went to bed early because I had nothing to do and did not wish to commence a letter to you as by the end of the week it would be so long that you never would take the time to decipher it, which you know would be an awful pity. I said I went to bed early. Lay there hour after hour, turning over first on one side then the other, fidgeting, scratching, kicking, rolling, and tumbling about just as one will you know when they are wakeful and have no one to talk to. After endureing it as long as I could, got up, sliped on my boots but did not dress, sallied forth in the night air, strolled about camp for half an hour, went back to bead, and actually got to sleep, but made up my mind I would not go to bed again to kill time. So to night there is no alternative but to write to you.

We heard from the regiment to day. They went to Nash[ville] last Sunday. Sunday night [they] drew horses for the whole regiment, and Monday morning bright and early started in persuit of Wheeler and Forest. We have Infantry stationed at the different fords along the Tenn. river, and it is the general opinion that their electioneering tour will be about as su[cc]essful as in all probability will be their candidate on the first of next month. I have just been reading a portion of the platform unanamously adopted by the Chicago convention—the principals which are to govern the affairs of this nation for the next four years if the "Democracy" are successful in the comeing elections. What thing indeed is moore wonderful than the tenacity with which apparently consciencious men (for I really think some of that party *are*

consciencious) still cling to the doctrine of constitutional guaranties in behalf of slavery, an institution which has inspired the most monstrous treason of all history.[1]
What man but is entirely blinded by party prejudice or is iminently dishonest and
traitorous will still be hesitating, after the experience of the past three years and a half,
to strike down every possible support of slavery? For however we may try to avoid
the fact, slavery (mind when I speak of slavery I mean the system of oppression practiced by the southern *gentleman*—not the negro, for the negro is no moore responsable
for this war than is the steel blade which the assassin plunges into the heart of his
victim responsable for the deed of murder) is the cause of all our troubles. Slavery
has struck at the life of the nation, and in self defen[ce] shal not the nation strike
down slavery? I would have slavery abolished not only by a proclimation of the chief
magistrate of the nation, not only as a war measure (I have not forgotten my position on this matter a year ago last spring, have you? But I repented of my sins and
turned from my iniquities and you have tacitly forgiven me), a military necessity, but
would have the constitution so amended that neither slavery nor involuntary servi-
tude except as punishment for crime whereof the parties shal have been duly convicted shal exist in the United State[s] or any place subject to their jurisdiction.[2] I
would have this a *free* country. It needs no argument other than common sense to
point the inconsistency of a *free* government resting even partially upon the basis of
slave labor. Now no longer does slavery really exist. Its own hand has struck down
the protecting shield of a constitutional guaranty, and all men feel that the condemnation is just. Now there is few "so poore to do it reverance." This is not strange. It
is the unif[orm] course and consequence of sin. The wicked prosper for a season,
but their end is nigh and their distruction sure. God has spoken at last in a voice that
we must hear, a vo[i]ce that resounds through out the Earth. It is the voice of war, a
voice [of] woe, of weeping, lamentation, and mourning—the voice of civil war, the
sum of woes. Slavery is now at our mercy, or rather its future is in our hands, and in
proportion as we mete out mercy to this acursed institution, we mete out inhuman-
ity to man and fearlessness to God. Slavery is destroyed, and shal we permit it to be
revived? The way is open before us so plain that all who will may see. Shal we walk
therein? Shal we throw off the shackles of prejudice and do our duty as rational intelligent beings, as men, as Christians? We shal be false to every inspiration of Christianity, philanthropy, and patriotism if we now fail to remoove *forever* the curse of
slavery from our land. The creature is dead but *may* revive. Let us bury it far beneath
the constitution—bury it so deep that it may not be reserected by any thing or power
under the whole Heavens. The time has come when the *spirit* of the constitution can
be carried out and the preamble to that instrument be *made a living fact: all men* are
born with certain inalienable righ[ts]; among these is life, *liberty,* and the persuit of
happiness.[3] Shal we let the oppertunity slip? Shal we let the golden moments pass
unimprooved? Shal we neglect so great a salvation? Or shal we not rather retain a
constitution for the guideance of this people which shall secure to us and our pos-
terity down to the latest generation the blessings of liberty and peace? Our week-kneed
dyspeptics, political dyspeptics I mean (you know those with poor digestion are apt

to make mountains of mole hills) will doubtless cry out that *that* would be an infringement upon the rights of a part of the citizens of the United States. Let me assure that unfortunate class that we need now no longer give guaranties to the
slaveholding interests. The Southern oligarchy have taken advantage of such as they
had. They have not hesitated to attack their sole protector. They have raised the frat-
ricidal hand to strike the death blow to our free institutions, and now all our obligations are at an end. And now that the time is come, let us not hesitate—secession
being stifled—to repeal the least provision of the organic law which may in any way
again bring up the question of slavery. I think we have at last learned a nobler virtue
than forbearance with evil. Slavery must disappear from our constitution and statute books, or this country dies. It may be many years in its death struggle, but its
dissolution is sure. And let him who can hesitate for a moment on this great subject
write himself dow[n] a traitor—for he is one. No patriot can now hesitate—no lover
of his country can hesitate in a time like this. And if three years of war and death,
mourning and desolation has not taught a man that this is the alternative, that this
is the question now really before the American people, that man does not deserve a
country and should not own stock in a free government. He is fit only to be ruled,
fit only for a slave. [There] is a clause in the constitution which guarantees the right
of the citizen[s] of each state the same privaledges a[s] in the several states. We know
that this section of the constitution has heretofore been practically a dead letter,
allthough we know it to be as fully a part of the supreme law of the land as that other
section for the condition of persons held to service![4] We know to[o] eq[u]ally well
the reason of it—it was concession to the fierce passion of slaveholding politicians,
the cowardly truckling to our *masters,* the lordly, overbearing Southerners who have
the dagger raised to strike us down as the reward of our years of vaselage. They refused to the people of the free states the same freedom of speach and the press that
was allowed in the free states to the people of the slave states. It was incendiary to
say a word in condemnation of the most stupendous fraud ever commited upon
humanity in any age, and this to[o] in a *free* country.[5] *Free* indeed must be [the] country which holds four millions of its subjects in the most abject slavery. For more than
half a century, one of the great principals of our boasted government has been a nullity.
Citizens of the United States have been subject to the grossest insult—have been tared
and feathered and burnt and hung and subjected to indignities without number and
without name. For more than thirty years we have submited—tamely submited to a
despotism less tolerant than the absolutism of ancient France or the moore ancient
autocracy (I guess that is the word to convey my meaning—it is derived from autocrat any way and *you* will know what I mean by it whether there is any such word in
the English language or not) of Russia.[6] For long years we have submited to these
outrages with the docility of slaves as we were, and it was only by the action of our
oppressors that we threw off this yoke. They forced us to vindicate our manhood or
submit, not only to slavery but to death. We chose the former, and I thank God for
the guardian care with which he has watched over us.[7] Though we have passed through

many dark valleys, though our skies have many times been over cast with clouds which seemed about to engulf us in midnight darkness, yet out of all these has God mercifully brot us. And now the morning is dawning bright and clear, and I believe the day is not far when we shal be permited to return to our friends and enjoy the blessings of quietude, having finished the work assigned us, that of the redeaming our dear country from her thraldom and a great people from the curse of slavery. It is now 12 o'clock and I must say good night, though I don't feel a bit sleepy. Think perhaps I will if I quit thinking and try. Once more Ellen good night.

1. In the 1864 election, the Republicans adopted a platform calling for the preservation of the Union and the abolition of slavery. The Democrats' platform called for peace, pronounced the Northern war effort a failure (they adopted that plank in late August just prior to the major Union victory at Atlanta), and promised to preserve the rights of the states. Most Northerners interpreted this last plank to mean that the Democrats would not act at the Federal level to abolish slavery.

2. Note the similarity to the wording of the Thirteenth Amendment to the Federal Constitution, then making its way through the U.S. Congress en route to the Northern states for ratification.

3. Squier confuses the language of the Declaration of Independence with that of the preamble to the U.S. Constitution.

4. The reference is to article 4, section 2.

5. In the antebellum decades white Southerners sought to stifle any criticism of slavery. Many Northerners saw this suppression of the civil liberties of whites as one of the main reasons for opposing the expansion of slavery.

6. The references are to the "absolute monarchy" of France before the overthrow of Louis XVI in 1789, and to the Russian czar, widely regarded as an absolute ruler. Ironically, in 1861 the czar used that power formally to abolish serfdom in Russia, as Squier noted in Letter 6.

7. Squier repeats the belief, widespread in the North in the antebellum decades, that the slaveholding South exercised undue control over the Federal government and used that power to run roughshod over the North, dominating the Northern representatives in Congress, pushing for the expansion of slavery into the Western territories, and threatening to establish absolute rule over the nation. This view was well expressed by a young Northerner who wrote that the Southern politicians "had trampled on the rights and just claims of the North sufficiently long and have fairly shit upon all our Northern statesmen and are now trying to rub it in and I think now is the time . . . for the North to take a stand and maintain it until they [sic] have brought the South to their [sic] present level." By seceding and starting a war, the Southerners had forced the Northerners to defend themselves, and, Squier believed, the Confederates deserved what they got as a result of their own actions. See Michael F. Holt, *The Political Crisis of the 1850s* (New York, 1978), especially 45–54.

LETTER 6

Chattanooga Oct. 13, 1864

Dear Ellen,

Hallalujah! All pr[a]ise and honor and glory to the loyal people of Indiana! The credit of the old Hoosier state is saved—Governor Morton is reelected![1] Freedom rejoices! And me thinks the Angles of Heaven clap their fair hands in ecstatic delight, and the hosts of Heaven raise one universal cry of joy! The children of men have spoken for human rights and liberty in a voice that reverberates throughout Earth and heaven! Honest men and patriots are joyous and encouraged! Devils tremble for the safety of their kingdom on earth (the southern confederacy). Treason has received a blow from which it may not recover, and traitors slink away into their holes where they will have time to consider their meanness, their worse than sinful course, and perhaps repent if repentence is for such vile creatures, which to my mind seems rather doubtful. Now no longer is the election of Abraham Lincoln a mooted point—it is a moral certainty, a foregone conclusion. Treason, the southern confederacy, and Slavery dies, and I rejoice at their dissolution. Freedom, human rights, liberty to all, and the pri[n]cipals of Christianity are become a living fact, a thing which really exists, and I thank God it is so. I thank God that the American people are awaking to their o[b]ligations to themselves, to humanity, to the world, and to the High and mighty Ruler of [the] Universe. Every day my confidence in human nature, in the inherent goodness of mankind, increases. Every day I see fresh evidence that man is not all bad, and every day I can but acknow[l]edge the goodness of our Great Father to his children. But this is morning and I must not get to spinning out nonsense now. Must wait until night, for then there will be no other way of killing time. But I felt so good over the election, I really could not help expressing myself to [y]ou *imediately.* Couldn't wait till night.

Oct. 15. For the past two days my eyes have been very sore so that I could neither read nor write, and the time has d[r]agged so heavily that it seemed allmost unendureable. They are not well yet, but I cannot resist the temptation to write a little while. As I told you, I tried to get my papers started up but without success. There can be nothing done but through the regular chanel. In fact, there would be no use starting them until communication is opened with Atlanta, as they have to be approved at department head quarters. Hood's whole fo[r]ce is now between this place and Sher[m]an, and it is uncertain when communication w[ill] be again established.[2] When the time comes, I shal act honorable if possable, dishonorable if I must.[3] Could it possably be arranged so that I could spend the winter. Wouldn't mind staying with Uncle Samuel until he gets out of his present troubles, but can't think of soldiring through these long dreary months. Well, my eyes have *giv[e]n* out, so I must quit.

16th. It is Sunday, and all [is] quiet, so I will scribble a few lines. The regiment came in last night, tired, hungry, and awful dirty. This morning they took th[eir] old position as [?], so there is but little doubt but they will stay here this Winter. The boys had rather a rough time and were very glad to get back home, and are now satisfied that they have been having an easy time here in Chattanooga. Before they went out it was quite common for them to wish to be to the front (that is t[he] new recruits). The duty was so hard here, they had to come on guard every other day, and have inspection Sundays, and all this kind of thing. I sometimes think it makes little difference how we are situated—we are sure to complain at our lot. Few men would be contented if they *had every thing they wanted.* The weather is fair and cool, without frost, and [my] health coul[d] not be better. I have not yet been able to draw pay. Think I shal wait and draw four months. Have not yet been relieved from the military commission—don't expect to be until I ask for it.

I think I agreed to give you a few thoughts on the subject [of] the constitution. So perhaps [I] might as well do so now as any tim[e], for you know that I would soon have to stop writing if I did not write about something. It is a subject upon which I think we do not exactly agree, but we differ so little. Perhaps when we know each other's views better we may agree perfectly. I consider the con[sti]tution the organic law of the nation, the foundation of our national e[xis]tence, the chief stone of the corner of our political edific, the indissolu[ble] bond of the Union and our liberties, the foundation of law and pol[it]ical o[r]der. And the man who knowingly violates its provisions merits the punishment that followe[d] the sacreligious touch of David's servant to the ark of the covenant—instant death.[4] The man who will raise the ruthless hand to des[troy] the foundation (though there may be some blocks of spurious marble in that foundation) of the noblest fabric of free government eve[r] founded upon Earth deserves to be cast into outer darkness. And the man who can stygmatize the framers of that instrument as old fogies [is] not moore loyal than he should be. Taki[ng] the circumstances with which they were surrounded into consideration (don't leave out the Slave oligarchy element for it ex[is]ted then as now), I consider it one of the grandest productions which has ever emenated from the uninspired mind. It was not per[f]ect nor need we look for perfection short of Inspiration. I will yiel[d] to none in my devotion to the Constitution. There are few who go befo[re] me in reverence for it, but I think the time has come under the providence of God for its *amendment* (not distruction). But in the mids[t] of the fierce conflict with traitors who has set at naught its binding force, let us be careful that in our zeal to punish the enemys of our government we be not guilty of a similar offence. Let us not be guilty of the same offence which [we] so condemn and rightly to[o] in others. Let us preserve the constitution unimpaired, but [in] God's name. Let us have it amended and imediately, but let it be done according to the provisions of that instrument. For it has within itself the propper way of effecting the desired change. It derives a great portion of its claim upon our regard from the fact that it recognizes the eternal law of progress. And while it establishes a government which should be [as] e[n]dureing as time, [this] does not assume that it has exha[u]sted the possibilities of the wants of future generations. It provides every facility for necessary ch[ange]. The framers of that instrument saw with something akin to insp[iration] that time and circumstances which make the politic[al] statesmanship of one period the exploded theory of the next. *They* knew that the science of politics was progressive—onward, ever onward towards perfection is the watch-word of all truly great minds. Political economy [of] civil Government (I did not intend making capital G there) is a philosophy that never rests, which has never attained its end, which is never perfect. Its law is progress. A point which yesterday was invisible is its goal to day and will be its starting point tomorrow. Viewing the matter as I do, we canot place to[o] high a [?] store upon the sagacity and wisdom of the fathers of the constitution. They saw that refermation is the watch-word of all history. Anarchy, distruction, and death is the fate of those nations which heed it not. This principal of progression may be stifled for a season, but in time it will speak in a voice that must be heeded. The Serfs of Russia endured its suppression for ages, and when about to break forth in its might, the old Autocrat, acting wisely, made a virtue of what would soon have been a necessity. The fath[ers] of this Republic wisely made provisions for this law of nature, and let us not be entirely unthankful for their care for our well being. Let us not foolishly throw away the only safeguard of our liberties. Let us not "curse our God and die"[5] because we may now be sorely afflicted. We may if we will come out of our troubles strengthened and purified. Thereby the mind of the American people to day occupies a higher moral state than ever before since we were a nation.

Long ere this reaches its destination you will know of the mighty struggle for existence that is now being made by the Southern Confederacy. You will know that Hood's whole army (now under comd. of Beurregard) [Beauregard] is in the *rear* of Sherman's forces.[6] That along the whole line of communication from Atlanta to Nashville, all is anxiety and excitement and preperation for the *worst*. Yet all are hopeful that the moove may proove the distruction of the confederate army. We will not beli[e]ve so dire a calamity as the evacuation of Atlanta and the falling back of Sherman possable. We know that to be the object of this bold moove of the enemy, and we wait with something akin to fear. A kind of feverish anxiety to hear the *very latest* news is seen where ever we go. Every feeling is bound up in the one idea—sucess to our armies and death and defeat of the enemy. Leaves and resignations are now impossable, and if they were not I would not disgrace myself and friends by asking for either *now* in a time of danger and trouble, for besides quitting the service of my country in its time of greatest need, it would appear cowardly. Thoug[h] I hold no pretension to bravery, I would not wish to be b[r]anded with cowardice. [I would] sooner by far die than that the world could say to my children your father was a coward. *He* left the service on the eve of a great battle. He served his country until the time of danger came, and then sneaked away. You may find some difficulty in reconciling this with what I wrote at some other time—"honorably if possable, if not dishonorably." I will explain. A man serves three years but within that time he is so unfortunate as to have received promotion. After having served faithfully for three long years, he wishes to return to civil life. Accordingly, in a time of general quiet when his services can best be spared, he sends up his unconditional resignation. Is there any thing wrong in that! He has served the term for which he enlisted. He has performed his contract with his government. His resignation goes up. In time he receives something like the follow[in]g: Special Orders No. ——— Capt. ——— is hereby dishonorably dismissed the service of the United States to date from ——— and signed Maj. Genl. Thomas. Is that man disgraced? Can one man simply by his declaration consign another to eternal infamy? Or does it not require some action upon the part of the man disgraced? In such a case I shall feel myself just as much a *man,* notwithstanding Genl. Thomas['s] declaration to contrary, as though I had stayed in the service for ten years (setting patriotism aside).

There is all manner of rumers afloat. One is Sherman is fighting at Dalton. Another that the[. . . .] is swinging around on Bridgport, and another that they are advancing in force upon this place.[7]

There is one thing sure—for the last forty eight hours there has been brisk preperation going on here for a fight. Artillery is placed in position, amunition served out to the men, fatigue parties working night and day building new works and strengthening old ones, beer saloons closed, and men ordered to stay with their respective commands. In short, if our erring brethren call on us they will receive a fitting reception. They will not find us sleeping. Well it is nearly 11 o'[c]lock and as I did not sleep much last [night] perhaps I had better adjourne. In fact, my eyes are not entirely well yet, though they are quite strong, for I have written nearly two pages on this large sheet without resting and with little fatig[u]e. Thoug[h] when I think about it, I feel that they will soon demand rest. The weather is fine. Nights just cool enough to be comfo[r]table with a little fire. We have a fireplace in our *sitting room.* Good night Ellen. Hope the time will soon come when I shal not have to *write* my good nights but can just give you kiss not such as we send on paper ——— thus but a real live warm kiss. I must close. Once moore, good night.

18th. Things are a little moore quiet now than for the past few days. Was talking with an old friend who was taken prisoner at Dalton and paroled. He came from the front to day and says that Sherman attacked and whiped the enemy severely yesterday.[8] He reports the road from here to Atlanta a perfect wreck and that it will take a month or six weeks to put it in running o[r]der. But our army has rations for one hundred days, so there is little danger of being compeled to fall back for want of subsistance. He was with the rebs two days and [a] half, and during that time had nothing to eat except a little parched corn and green cane stalks which was found in the country through which they marched. Said he did not feel lik[e] complaining as he fared as well as his captors. It was Hood's intention to fall suddenly upon our depots along the line and capture large quantities of supplies, but in this he was foiled. He is now far from his base without subsistence and his army badly demoralized, with an implacable foe upon his rear and flanks. Such now *appears* to be the case. Time alone can proove the truth or falsity of this view. We wait with something of impatience the issue of the stupendous military opperations now in progress both here and in the east. Grant appears to be closing around Richmond, and I firmly beli[e]ve that before the 8th day of next month the glorious old flag will float over the capital of the confeder[a]cy and Grant's Head quarte[rs] will be the capitol in Richmond.

Latest accounts here from Indian[a] puts Morton's majority at thirty thousand. That's pretty fair for on[e] of the strongest democratic states in the union. And Pennsylvani[a], that life long democratic state, has spoken for the union and the suppression of treason.[9] What do our democratic brethren think about their chance of success at the November election? What do they now find to buoy up their spirits in their distress? The one comfort they have, one friend that will stick to them throug[h] evil report, a balm for their every wound, a sovereign remedy for disappointed politicians and the whole family of McLellanites. The internal revenue tax makes it rather expensive. A tax of 75 cts. pr. gal. on corn whiskey is certainly an untold outrage on the democracy. In fact, I don't know but it is sufficient cause for them to secede from the government of Father Abraham. Surely ten cents a drink for "rot gut" is awful. How will they endure it, poor fellows? It is to[o] bad, but I would not for my life help them if I could. But if I cannot write something with a *little* sense I had better *adjourn.* Must close this up to night, for it must certainly go to office tomorrow morning, else you may have to go two weeks without a letter. I sometimes think I would give a pretty thing to know whether you care to read my allmost interminable and prosy letters. I know you like long letters, but [not] whether you like such awful long ones when one has so little to write about. I never go out of sight of my quarters, never see anything new or strange to discribe of. It is of no use to write general news, for that you get long before we do down here. So there is no alternative but to write whatever I may hapen to be thinking about. That might do if I possessed the faculty of expressing the ideas properly. I of course might make some improovement in that line by making corrections, but the fact is I have not the patience to read over my letters after writing them. If I would, no doubt but you would receive rather shorter comm[u]nications, as much of my scribbling would then be deposited in its proper place under the firestick in a bright fire. That puts me in mind of the fact that the fire is allmost entirely out and my feet are really cold. So I will go to bed to keep from freezing. Good night darling. Heaven bless and preserve you all. Give a kiss to little Ella, Allice, and Wilber for papa, and my love to my good dear kind mother. God bless her and keep her from harm. It pains me to know that father persecutes her so for her political sentiments.[10] Blessed are ye when men shal persecute you for my sake or for the sake of right.[11] Ever your own

George

1. Unionists carried the October state elections, reelecting Governor Morton with 152,084 votes to 131,201 for the Democrats' Joseph E. McDonald.

2. After the fall of Atlanta, Gen. John Bell Hood's Confederate army that had been defending that city maneuvered around to wreck the railroad between Atlanta and Chattanooga. The Federal army, under the command of Maj. Gen. William T. Sherman, had captured Atlanta, pursuing the Rebels northward and then west into Alabama. The Army of the Cumberland was part of Sherman's force.

   The rules of military bureaucracy required paperwork such as Squier's (furlough? resignation?—see below in this letter) to be processed "through channels." The papers had to pass through the headquarters of the Army of the Cumberland, and its headquarters were with the army in Georgia.

3. See below in this letter.

4. See 1 Chron. 13:9.

5. See Job 2:9.

6. Gen. John Bell Hood commanded the Confederate army that had moved against the Chattanooga–Atlanta railroad. Hood soon swung westward across north Alabama. Gen. P. G. T. Beauregard had been put in command of the Rebel forces in the Deep South. Although he later visited Hood's army in Alabama, Beauregard did not assume direct command. See note 8 to this letter.

7. There was occasional skirmishing as Hood struck at the railroad before moving westward into Alabama.

8. Hood's Confederates attacked the Federal garrison at Dalton, Georgia, thirty-eight miles from Chattanooga, on October 13. The Union commander surrendered. The white officers of the garrison were paroled on the fifteenth. The black Union soldiers of the garrison were put to work tearing up the railroad. Several were shot by the Confederates. See OR, 39, pt. 1, 719–23. No significant fighting occurred on October 17.

9. See note 1 above. The October vote in Pennsylvania was 249,959 Unionist; 236,061 Democratic.

10. An oblique and fascinating comment. Unfortunately, nothing is known of her sentiments other than what appears here.

11. See Matt. 5:11.

LETTER 7

Chattanooga Dec. 5, 1864

Darling,

It has now been nearly two weeks since the rct. of your last letter and O! how heavily time hangs but we expect mail tomorrow and then I am sure of hearing from those who are dearer to me than all the world beside. How very often do I dream of being at home and every thing seems so natural. Then I wake up homesick and low spirited and wish it was not me or at least that I was at home where one can enjoy life, not ease, but the society of those I love. For the past 10 days all communication North has been severed—no mail nor northern papers. We do not even as much as hear from Thomas's Army. One day has it that Hood is routed and hotly persued by our victorious army, the next day perhaps Thomas is defeated and has fallen back within the defences of Nashville.[1] But I very much doubt whether there has been any fighting to amount to much during the whole campaign.[2] Sherman is said to be march[ing] on towards the Gulf with but little opposition.[3] All is conjecture and nothing a certainty. One thing is very sure—the present moovements must be attended with stupendous results. If successful, a great thing is accomplished; if unsuccessful, dire is the calamity which is upon us. I sometimes think of the French expedition to Moscow[4] and tremble for Sherman's safety. But I think there is power above man's power which will uphold him, a wisdom above man's wisdom which will direct and guide him to victory. Let us hope for the best and pray God that he may be successful.

Genl. Steedman[5] with all the troops at this post except the 44 & 29 Ind. is down the river somewhere but *where* we do not know. He has several colored regiments which experience has taught us is to be relied upon in any emergency. I have got an overcoat like unto those you have at home. Allso another pr. pants and several prs. drawers, enough so that I can give two pr. when I get home. I can get Government clothing here for a mere fraction of what similar articles cost up in America. I just counted my Green backs in order to keep you posted up on the state of my finances, and I have just $174.95, exclusive of a few postage stamps. To day I squandered 15 cts., the first since pay day. There was some apples on the street. The temptation was greater than I could bear and I fell. I don't know whether I told you the change in our domestic affairs on the reorganization of the company. I made a copl. of an old cook, Chet Markham,[6] and took in another boy which we like very much—one of my favorites. His name is Thomas Trittips and is from Langrange Co.[7] I find the change decidedly advantagous. He is neat and remarkably economical, which at present prices of subsistance is quite an item. I have since last payday only paid out for rations about $10. You may think strange how this can be. It is told in a few words. We have a first rate orderly and he boards at Head Quarters. The rations all pass through his hands. We save a part of what would otherwise be thrown away by the men. We eat very little pork, as there is none t'all issued to the men and one can't afford to buy much at 25 cts. pr. pound. I expect Stowe's[8] Commission here in a few days when I have the assurance of going home. Shell's trial has not come off yet.[9] My health is good. I must close this for the present, as the candle is [al]most out, so good night.

Dec. 27. Nearly a month has elapsed since I commenced on this sheet, and during that time I have had no word from [?] for obvious reasons. You may think strange that after so long a time since the date of my last that I cannot give you a good long old fashioned letter, so I will explain. By request of Col. Com.[10] I was relieved from military commission and have been on duty in charge of Guards every other day and night ever since. You know very well the effect of loss of sleep—dull, lifeless, and half dead. To day got your note of 30 ult. It is scarcely necessary for me to explain why I am stil in Chatt[anooga]. As soon as the trains run through to Nashville an officer will start for Indianapolis for the commission. I am entirely sick of staying here. Will leave at the earliest possable moment. I will not set the time again for fear I may be againe dis[a]ppointed. My helth is good. O! Yes, right. I must mention my Christmas. The Non Com Staff of the regiment got up as fine a dinner as any to which I ever sat down. Pies, cakes, sauces, chicken, pickles, &c&c, all served up in excellent stile. The Col., Lt. Col., Adjt., Maj. Rerick, and "your very humble Servt." composed the favored few at the first table.[11] Every thing passed off finely. After concluding the meal we all filled not our glasses but cups with coffee (not wine) and drank to the health of the "non com Staff of the 44th," after which the segars were passed around, and went on our way rejoiceing. Where New Year's will find me of cours I cannot tell. Would have given $50 to have been at home during the holidys. Weather warm, rainy, and disagreeable. Streets awful muddy. My love to all, especially your own dear self. As ever you own

George W. Squier

1. Communications between Chattanooga and Nashville were out because the Confederates, who had moved north from Georgia, had advanced through Alabama into middle Tennessee and, by December 5, 1864, were just south of Nashville. They cut the railroad between that city and Chattanooga.
2. One of the most terrible battles of the war took place at Franklin, Tennessee, on November 30, between Hood's army and part of Thomas's forces.
3. In mid-November 1864, Sherman abandoned his pursuit of the Confederates into Alabama and returned to Atlanta. After destroying that city, Sherman's troops marched into the interior of Georgia. His destination was Savannah, on the Atlantic Coast, not the Gulf of Mexico.
4. The reference is to Napoleon I's 1812 campaign into Russia. The vast distances and the onset of winter turned the expedition into a disaster for Napoleon's French army.
5. Maj. Gen. James B. Steedman commanded the District of the Etowah that embraced the Chattanooga area as well as large sections of north Alabama and north Georgia.
6. Chester Markham of Rome veteranized and served with the regiment until mustered out September 14, 1865, as a sergeant.
7. Thomas S. Triphito of Haw Patch, a recruit, joined the regiment on March 9, 1864. He served until mustered out September 14, 1865, as a corporal.
8. Sylvester J. Stowe of Pleasant Lake was commissioned first lieutenant on February 11, 1865, and served until mustered out with the regiment. He had originally enlisted with the company in 1861.
9. No details of this trial are known, but Shell remained on duty with the regiment until January 28, 1865, when he was mustered out at the end of his original term of service. Letters 5 and 7 in chapter 2 may shed some light on this episode.
10. James F. Curtis was colonel of the regiment, but this may refer to some other officer then commanding the post or the garrison.
11. The lieutenant colonel of the regiment was Philip Grund of Fort Wayne. The adjutant was Samuel E. Smith of Elkhart.

Chapter 4. 1865

ℰℐ

LETTER I

[Chattanooga]

Thursday, Feb. 23 [1865]. Rain all night last night and all day and still it rains, and what is worse, the Sergt. Major just stuck his head in at the doore and blabed out "Capt. Squier on picket tomorrow." O! Yes, last night I forgot to mention quite an item in tra[n]sactions of the day. In yesterday morning's paper there appeared an order from Gen. "Jim" [Steedman] that there be a national salute fired in honor of the event of the evacuation of Charleston and the hoisting of the American flag over Fort Sumpter. Accordingly, at 12 all the bells of the town comenced ringing, and soon the guns from every hilltop and Fort surrounding Chattanooga took up the chorus, and the echos of their thunders reverberated among the hills and ravines of Missionary Ridge and sent back from the mighty walls of Old Lookout, and floating along the valley of the Tennessee conveyed to the dwellers in mountains and plains the joyous tidings that another and the worst strong hold of treason and perjury had fallen before the might and power of the union arms. To union men and women this terrific thunder was sweet music, and they rejoiced in it. But to the rebels it must have seemed the death knell of their unholy Confederacy, bidding them to put their house in order and prepare for its early decease.[1] Vicksburg fell on the 4th of July, 1863; Savannah was a Christmas present in 1864;[2] the celebration of the fall of Charleston was the aniversary of the birth day of the Father of this Country;[3] and who will say but the 4th of March may alike be celebrated as the day on which Abraham Lincoln is inaugurated President of the United States and the fall [of the] Rebel capital? Let us work with h[e]art and brain, not forgetting our dependence upon the High and Mighty ruler of the universe. And may we not hope that the anniversary of the birth day of these United States may witness the total prostration of the demon secession? Surely the end[. . . .]

1. The Confederates evacuated Charleston, South Carolina, during the night of February 17–18, 1865. Northerners looked upon the city where the first secession convention had

met in December 1860 as the birthplace of the rebellion. The Federals were especially glad to regain possession of Fort Sumter ("Sumpter" was a frequent misspelling), which the secessionists had captured in April 1861 at the start of the war. See Rerick, *The Forty-fourth Indiana Volunteer Infantry*, 117–18.

2. Sherman had finished his march across Georgia by capturing Savannah on December 21, 1864. He then presented the city metaphorically to President Lincoln as a Christmas present.

3. News of the capture of Charleston reached Chattanooga on February 22 (George Washington's birthday), 1864.

LETTER 2

Head Qrs. Co. "D" 44th Ind. Inft. Chattanooga March 12th, 1865

Dear Ellen,

This morning's mail bro[ugh]t me your two last letters written at Pioneer dated I think 27th ult. and March 4th in which you wrote that you intended starting home in a few days. Perhaps I may have done wrong in not directing another letter either to Pioneer or Williams Center, but I did not care to run much risk of their falling into other hands than those for which they were intended. Perhaps I am different from most people about that. I never want *outsiders* to my letters, and I never read for the benefit of the public the letters I receive from my friends. Of course, I do not object to your reading my letters or parts of them to such of your friends as you may see fit, but I should not feel free to express myself to our friends at large as freely as to you. I may seem rather foolish to write two letters in such quick succession, and I most assuredly should not do so if it were not to acknowledge the receipt of your [letter] from Pioneer. Can you doubt that your letters are a *great comfo[r]t* to me? If you do doubt it I am sure I know of no means of convincing you. I can only say that they are not only a *great comfort* but they are allmost my *only* source of real enjoyment. Were it not for them, I really believe I should die of the blues. Many, very many times during the cold months that have passed I have thought of you and how much you must suffer, and from the bottom of my heart have I pitied your desolate condition. All along I was in hopes that I would be permited to at least visit you, but all the long winter nights are past. Spring is now here, and when at last the time came that I could be spared from the company nearly as well as not, I am denied the pleasure of even a short visit at home, not by the officers of the regiment, but by higher authority. My application has not been returned disapproved, but without doubt it will in a few days, for if the request was granted it would have come around before this time. Well all that I can do is simply to submit. My eternal presence with my company may be necessary, but I certinly fail to see it. There is now three officers in my company and consquently I could be spared just as well as not. The weather to day is delightful, to[o] pleasant to stay in camp, but I had a job of fatigue for the company this morning and of course had to be present in order to have it suit, and this evening we had inspection and dress parade. Putting all togeather, I was compeled to stay in camp all day, not even going down town to church. As I don't "feel" for writing this evening I might as well close by sending a kiss to our little pets, and ask Ella if she still likes pa pa "just as well as she does anyboddy." Ever your own

George W. Squier

LETTER 3

Chattanooga April 15, 1865

Dear Ellen,

As you will remember, I left home on the 6th. Had quite a pleasant drive with Dr. G.[1] Arrived at Fort Wayne about 10 o'clock and imediately proceeded to business. The garden seeds cost from 10 to 15 cts. pr. package. I could find no onion seeds in town. The coloring of W's pants cost $1.00, his vest $3.00, hoe $1.00. the silk $1.56, Nitrate 10 cts., and Ella's doll head 45 cts, a ridding comb for myself 30 cts., and the two prs. boots $21.00, and a valice for Lieut. Casebeer $5.00.[2] Took supper with Charlotte and left all of the things which I had bought for you. At 5 o'clock, left C.'s,

Members of the 44th Indiana Volunteer Infantry in camp at Chattanooga, Tennessee. Courtesy of Bob Willey.

checked my bagage through to Indianapolis, and in twenty minutes I had really started for the "Sunny South." The coaches were crowded but after standing for a short time got a seat faceing a man and wife with a small child and a little girl about seven years old. The latter occupied a seat with me. The man was rather intelligent appearing and I felt like talking to some one, so I remarked that it was a pleasant day though rather coll [cold]. "Yes." We are receiving glorious news from the army. "Very good." The war may now be considered virtually at an end. "Yes that is the general opinion." I went on talking about the realtive strength of the two armies and the utter imposability of the rebels holding out longer than a few months, but could only succeed in eliciting monosylables, [and th]en only in reply, and then only to direct [questions]. I did not like to give it up so, and turning to the little girl at my side asked her name, age, wher she lived, where she was going, &c, stroked her hair back, patted her cheek, and *may* have remarked that she was *pretty*. And of course, saw strikeing resemblence to the mother (what man is there which does not like to hear his wife complimented). And of cours, the little boy on his mother's lap "looked like his father." I had touched the right cord. He was entirely throw[n] of[f] his guard. In fact, he was surprised and surrendered unconditionally, for I really belive he had fully made up his mind to be as unsociable as possable. At any rate, after that I found him quite agreeable, and passed off the time quite pleasantly until we arrived at Perue, where we arrived at 9 o'clock. No train until 5 in the morning, so I took the "Buss" to the hotel, paid half a dollar for a bed, and turned in but could not get to sleep until late, though I had a good bed in a nice airy room. It is now just 2 o'clock P.M. and the news is just received that President Lincoln and Sect. Seward was last night assassinated.[3] Every flag in town and on fortifications is at "half mast." Everything is quiet. Little knots of men and officers are to be seen in every direction converseing in subdued voices. Those who are walking around have solemn faces and moove with easy tread, as though they were conscious of haveing lost their greatest and best friend. I feel that this [is] so, yet there are thousand[s] at the *North* who will *rejoice* at the dire calamity which has come upon this nation.

Evening. I feel very, very sad to night. One of the first men of the land has been cowardly assassinated. But will it stop here? Or is this only the beginning of a long series of dark deeds? Is it possable that this is the beginning of a second "Reign of Terror?" God preserve this land from such a calamity. But I cannot but fear the worst. Just now a friend drops in for an evening chat, so I must adjourne.

Sunday. Trators and assassins have again aroused the just indignation of the American people. Like a thunder-clap in a clear sky came the announcement that "Abraham Lincoln is dead—killed by an assassin." Men were struck dumb, their senses completely paralized. But now that they can think, there goes up one universal cry of *vengence, death, extermination* to *all* traitors.

> Away! Away! We will not hear
> Of aught save death a vengence now
> By the Eternal skies we swear

Our knees shal *never* learn to bow
We will not hear a word of peace
Nor grasp in friendly grasp a hand
Linked to the traitor's race
That work the ruin of our land.[4]

The feeling of regret for our loss is not all unmixed with hatred, not only for the fiend who has robed us of our leader, the Saviour of our country, but for the whole class both North and South who are rejoiced at our loss. We look anxiously for the development of the policy of President Johnson. But who that knows his past history can doubt but there will be even moore vigorous measures adopted than has characterised the administration for the past four years?[5] May there be no hesitation! No faltering, no terms with traitors, murderers, assassins—talk not to me of the honor [of] Robert E. Lee[6] and the boasted chivelry of "Southern Gentlemen." As soon look for honor among the inhabitants of a climate *many* degrees warmer than the "Sunny South." Let the war go on; let there be no terms but unconditional surrender; let a hundred lives of our "erring Brethren" be sacrificed for every drop of blood which has been so ruthlessly spilled. The sooner the world is rid of those vile creatures, the better it will be for mankind. Enough of this truckling to the unprincipaled fiends—it is taking the deadly viper in from the cold and warming it to life, only to be stung to death with its venomous fangs. The friends of the Southern Confederacy may contend that the leaders of the rebellion are not respo[n]sable for the act. Away with such "stuff." The plot was concocted in the Confederate Capital, and Jefferson Davis and Robert E. Lee were the originators.[7] They are responsable for the murderous deed. They and theirs should suffer there for let[ting] the war go on. Ask them not to lay down their arms and return to their allegiance. Extirminate—yes that is the word—let *extirmination* be our watchword, and death to *all* traitors our war cry. We now have our foot upon the neck of our enemy. Let us wreak a sweet revenge. Let them pay the penalty of their sins! Let['s] avenge not only this one great wrong, but the lives of three hundred thousands of our brothers who have fallen in this cruel war. You may think that I do not exhibit a remarkably mild spirit. I confess that I [am] not an angel of goodness. There is a point where forbearance and mercy seaces to be a vir[t]ue, and in my very humble opinion we have now arrived at that point. For [in] ancient times men and nations became so extremely wicked that God saw fit to use means to destroy them from the face of the Earth. May it not be the case with the late southern Confederacy. I am free to admit that I think it is, and if so let me say that I am willing to be an humble instrument in my very humble way in assi<st>ing to bring about the desired end. I have written quite enough on this strain. At any rate, this sheet is greatly filled and [it] certainly will not pay to commence on a new sheet, as without doubt I should not know when to stop. It is rather difficult to make my mind to go on with the accou[n]t of my trip through to this, but perhaps after commencing I shal get along better than it now seems possible. At all events, it shal be my task to try. Of cours, you can not care to hear my prating upon what I consider the proper policy now to be adopted by our Government, especially when I feel as vengeful as I do at present. Doubtless time may modify my feelings on this subject, but at present I cannot see that I am wrong.

Sunday night, April 16th. If I mistake I left at Perue just after going to bed. Well, at 4 o'clock in the morning was waked up. Went dow[n] to the depot and at 5 started for Indianapolis. Procured a seat by myself in a first class coach and felt quite comfortable though rather dozy. Stoped at Kokomo for Breakfast wich cost 75 cts. Arrived at Indianapolis about 10 o'clock, nearly an hour after the train had left for Louisville. Put up at the Spencer house (you know, *we* stoped there the time you came down to Indianapolis with me in the fall of '62). Took dinner and Supper at 75 cts. pr. meal. 10 at night—started for Louisville. The car not crowded, so I had a seat to myself u[n]til we got to Seymore, where there was several laydis got aboard, and one of them without invitation or even permission *plonked* herself down at my side. At first I felt rather out of humor about the intrusion as I was very sleepy and wanted to curl down and if possable get a little rest. After a while getting over my "fit" thought I would enter into conversation with the "beautiful thing in Crinoline" (she would weigh I should think not far from 220 avoirdupois [?].) I remarked that it was rather u[n]pleasant traveling at night; no answer. "Do you reside in this vicinity?" Narry word. Determined not to be beat I said "Are you going as far south as Jeffersonville?" At the word Jeffersonville she looked up in my face (and such a look "me thinks I see it still") and answerd in the following beautiful and truly poetical words, *"Yah."* Of course I was *sold* and not at private sale, for in the seat directly to the rear I heard sounds which sounded to me wonderfully like a smothered laugh. In fact, it was decidedly a giggle. I see that I was "in for it," so I put my hand lightly upon my fair traveling companion's shoulder in order to attract her attention. She imediately looked (such an angelic face). I simply said "Sacre trappo houne Shistr."[?] She tur[n]ed indignantly away without attempting an answer. My friends in the back seat made some remark to me, but I did not feel like conversing. So I leaned my head against the back of the seat and *dozed.*

Arrived at Jeffersonville at 5 in the morning. Took the "buss" for Louisville and stoped at the National Hotel, a very good house at $4.00 pr. day. On inquiry I found that the Nashville train had left and that the next train left 2 ½ P.M., so of course I had to "lay over" until that time. As it is now bed time I think I will *lay over* in my bunk. So good night Nellie.

Monday night, April 17th. As you know before you read this, I spent a part of the time, a *very small* part, while waiting for the train writing a few lines to you, but neglected to drop the letter in the office. Time draged wearily along, but 2 o'clock finally came and I started on my way, if not rejoiceing, glad to get away from the city. My traveling companion was a Maj. Smith of the 6th Ind. Cavalry—sociable, well informed, and of *course* if he was well informed he was an *abolitionist* (not that *all* abolitionists are decidedly intellectual, but all smart *good* men I think are).[8] For the first Sixty miles everything went off very smoothly, but there at a way station (I don't remember the name) the conductor received notice that a bridge a few miles in advance was out of order and would not be repaired in less than four hours. So the Maj. and I went up to a private house a short distance, engaged supper, set by [a] good warm fire until it was ready, eat, paid half a dollar each, and at 9 o'clock we were again under headway. It was saturday night, and as the tra[n]sportation office would be closed on Sunday, I suggested to my traveling companion that we stop off at Cave City (which is just half way between Louisville and Nashville) until 12 the next day. At that place you know I opened this letter which should have been left at Louisville, wrote a few lines, but as there was no P.O. [post office] at that place, was obliged to carry it on to Nashville. Sunday at 12 we left for Nashville, where we arrived about 6 in the evening. Put up [at] the St. Cloud which is called a first class hotel but which is not as good as a third class country tavern—the clerks cross and crabid, the waiters careless and indifferent, the meals miserably cooked and served up, and every thing showed signs of the most gross neglect—table linnen dirty, glasses dirty, floors most awful dirty, walls blackened with smoke and dust, windows highly ornamented with cobwebs, and of course the bed was not the cleanest and most sweet that I had seen. But I lived through it, and after paying $5.00 pr. day, I was heartily glad to take the 2 o'clock train for this place, where I arrived next morning at 7. Left my baggage at the depot and walked up to camp. The boys appeared delighted to see me. They was "so glad to see me." They had been "so very lonesome" and it seemed "so long since I left" and they was "afraid I would stay over my time" &c. The Col. said he had not expected me so soon. It would have been just as well if I had staid at home the ballance of that week, but then I did not *know* and thought it best to be on the safe side. You may wish to know wheather I am as *blue* as I usually am after leaving home. I am not. One reason is doubtless the excitement of the news. You know, great events have followed in such quick succession for the past twenty days that one is allmost bewildered. Scarcely were we done rejoiceing over the fall of Richmond before the *Great* Robert E. Lee surrendered himself and his army,[9] and the reverberation of the thunder of artillery fired in honor of that occasion had scarce died away among the hills ere the heart sickning news of the death of our President flashed along the wires, causing every loyal heart to throb with paine. I do not know how it is among civilians, but allmost every soldier feels he has lost a near and dear friend. George Washington was the Father of his country. Abraham Lincoln was the Saviour of our nation. George Washington done all that there was for him to do and done it well. Abraham Lincoln done no moore and perhaps may have done his work no better, but who would compare the amount done by the former with that of the latter? He may have ered in some things, yet I consider him one of the greatest men the world has ever produced. But I will stop right here, as I did not intend [and] will not now eulogize the "mighty fallen." It is now ten o'clock and perhaps later, and I do not wish to get in the habit of keeping late hours (for you know that candle light is rather expensive). I may as well quit now as any time. But for some cause I would so much rather write at night than during the day. All through the day there is continually some one comeing in or going out and making so much noise that it is utterly impossable for me to think. And of course, one cannot write if they cannot think of anyth[in]g. O! Yes, now I think of it. If Mr. Spencer enquires about his boy, you tell him that I saw Albert at Nashville and delivered the Stockings and letters.[10] He is looking remarkably well and apparently enjoying himself very well. Good night.

Tuesday night, April 25. Though I was on duty yesterday and last night, I do not feel sleepy, and as the boys have gone to bed I can do nothing else but scribble a few lines. I do not know that I told you that there was several men arrested for expressing pleasure at hearing of the death of President Lincoln. There is, I believe, nine in all—four Soldiers and five citizens and Government Employees. Since their arrest they have been kept at work on the public works about town. Upon the back of each is a tin plate with the words "Assassin Sympathisers" painted in large letters. A few days since the Pro Mar [Provost Marshal] took them under guard to an artist and had their Photos taken in a group, the plate being placed on the breast instead of on the back as when at work. The picture is a nice thing, and if I was not so poor I would send one home that you might hang it up in your room for the benefit of some of our "erring b[r]ethren" at the North. Some of them who were ashamed of their position look as if they had eaten something very sower, green persimons for instance, and that the fruit didn't agree with them, while others carry a bold front as determined to make the best they can of a bad bargain. Lieut. Rivenburg,[11] Pro Marshal, purposes sending one of thes[e] pictures with the names of the individuals and a history of their case to Frank Leslie and have it reproduced in his pictorial, thus publishing to the world the shame of thes[e] *very patriotic* "peace on any terms" men. I have taken some pains to enquire into the previous history of these men, and as far as [I] can learn the[y] all voted for George B. McClellan for President. It is hardly necessary to tell this, as one would take it as a matter of course for we know that he was the traitor's candidate.

There is every indication of a moove of a portion of the troops from this post. Who the lucky ones will be, I have no means of knowing, nor whither they will go. The 4th Corps are still passing through this place on their way to some point north. Their baggage is all marked "Louisville, Ky."[12] I'll go to bed and try to sleep. Good night Darling.

April 27th. For the past two days I have been at work very hard putting up a new house which is 9 by 14 feet and very pretty. Of course, we used old refuse lumber, but for all that it is the best "shebang" in the regiment. To day I received your letter written soon after the receipt of the news of President Lincoln. You wanted to know the general feeling of the soldiers on this subject. If I mistake not, I anticipated that request in my last which was m[a]iled a week since. Now every one is wondering at the late action of Genl. Sherman. Most of the soldiers doubt his loyalty. He has suddenly fallen from among the first men of the nation to a poor despisable wretch.[13] Perhaps you know that he was never a great favorite with me. I have had men get mad when I told them that Genl. Rosecrans had given better evidence of superior Generalship than the much lauded Sherman. Sherman commenced his "briliant carer" one year ago by starting out on the great Atlanta Campaign with a sup[eri]or force of ve[te]ran troops, which enabled him to flank the enemy in his strong positions, and allso to keep his whole line directly in the enemy's f[r]ont intact, thus compeling him to fall back. And with all these advantages, nothing but the desperate fighting of his men saved a disastrous defeat at the battle of peach tree creek.[14] On the 22nd of July last he finally gained Atlanta and went into camp.[15] In time he telegraphed Genl. Grant that Hood was swinging round his right flank in order to get in his rear, thus endeavoring to sever communication and compel a retrogade moovement. Genl. Grant imediately dispatched a special mesenger with orders that he Sherman would imediately send Thomas with the 4th and 23rd corps back to Nashville to p[r]otect the rear, and that he Sherman would imediately march through Ga., making Savannah his objective point.[16] He obeyed order[s]. He acomplished his work, but without meeting the enemy in any force. And for this he has been lauded to the skies, termed the greatest military genious of the age. Genl. Rosecrans moved on Chattanooga with forty thousand men and by st[r]ateg[ly] compeled Bragg with a force of not less than Sixty thousand men to evacuate his strong hold and fall back, where he received reenforcments to the amount of not less than twenty thousand men, which [was] half the strength of Rosecrans whol[e] army. The battle of Chickamauga was fought with a loss of Eighteen Thousand men in killed, wounded, and missing.[17] The field was lost, but Chattanooga was taken *and held,* and for *this* he was reli[e]ved from the command of the army of the Cumberland. If Genl. Rosecrans with an army of two hundred thousand men had attacked Bragg in his strong hold and after Six months hardship and exposure had carried the place with a loss of a hundred thousand lives, he would have been lionised throughout [the] land as a great and sucessful Generel. As it was, he was not only extremely incompetent but a *coward* and wholely unfit to command an army in an active campaign. He was relieved with disgrace and assigned a command which should have been given to some second class colonel. And for this gross injustice he is indebted to the unprincipaled but once popular Genl. Halleck.[18] But I *will* quit this subject, as I k[n]ow it cannot interest you. It is so natural for me to write anything which happens to come into my mind without even a thoug[t] of whether it will interest you or not. I sometimes allmost promise myself that I will quit writing just to pass off the time until bed time. If [I] were in active service there might be something to write about, but here there is nothing going on, no changeing scenery, no stiring events, nothing out of the regular course transpireing, each day passing like the preceding one with remarkable sameness, which perhaps you cannot underst[an]d. Of course there are little incidents, but they would interest none but their imediate friends. So you see I have but very little *material* for writing in the common way.

Yester[day] at 2 o'clock P.M., John M. Gustine breathed his last—cause of death, Typhoid fever.[19] He was first attacked with rheumatism [and] sent to the hospital, where [he] partially recovered. In fact, he got so much better that he requested [the] Surg. in charge to send him back to his company. But the Dr. told him he had better stay a few days longer until he got entirely well. But poor fellow, he was attacked with the deadly fever, which carried him off in a few days. His brother was with [him] mo[s]t of the time for the last two days.[20]

Troops continue to pass through this place for some point North. I really am puzzeled to understand the present moovement, unless Johnston is expected to take a westerly direction, which seems quite probable.[21] I think I answered your letter or the most of it about the time you was writing it. In regard to the cost of the things, I did as near as I could remember at the time of writing, and it was not far from correct. If you had been *really disappointed* at the result of [a] certain little transaction which you may not have forgotten, you would not have been *the only one*. For the fact is I have often fou[n]d myself *allmost*—yes, moore than allmost—really wishing that it might be so.[22] But it is bed time and I must quit. It is really to[o] bad to send so much blank paper but this must go tomorrow morning else you may not get it next week. Kiss my little pet, my little Lady, and my dear good little man for me. Good night Darling. I think of you *very* often.

G.W. Squier

Co. "D" 44th Ind. Inft.

Tuesday night, May 2nd. Have bee[n] busy all day finishing up my muster rolls, drawing and issueing clothing to the men. This evening on dress parade we received orders to hold our commands in readiness to march at a moment's warning with five days' rations. But for all that I think there is little danger of leaveing here for several days, though of course there may be something in the wind that we understrapers know nothing about. But I can hardly think that we will go any farther South. You will perceive by the date that the first page on this sheet was written several days ago. I had calculated to sent it out last week, but forgot it until I run across it to day by chance. Well, there is no use trying to write to night, so here's a *kiss*.

Wednesday, May 3rd is decidedly pleasant. There is quite a stir about the supposed move. The probability is that if we leave this place we will go south, perhaps to Rome or Atlanta, Ga. There was a man of Co. "I" marched through camp with a placard on his back upon which was printed in large letters "This man wishes that President Lincoln and Col. Hodges are in hell where all officers should be." He was escorted by a strong guard which was the only thing that saved his life. Several times the cry was raised "hang him, hang him," and nothing but the firmness of the guards prevented the men from administering stern justice on the spot. After marching him around the parade ground twice he was sent to the military prison to await trial. Henry Kessler's sentence has finally come. It is that he be "discharged the service of the United States without Final Statements," which is the same as being discharged with the loss of all pay and allowances. He appears to be satisfied, but it is severer than I had expected. I shal get his discharge as soon as possable, for I know he is anxious to get home. He has acted foolishly, but he has been severely punished. "The way of the transgressor is hard," especially in the army [as] is this the case.[23] Some have a holy horror of any thing which savors of military power[. . . .]

1. "G." is unidentified other than by context. The reason for Squier's home visit is unknown. He probably was on furlough.

2. John E. Casebeer was mustered into the regiment as a corporal, reenlisted as a veteran, and was promoted second lieutenant, February 17, 1865. See Rerick, *The Forty-fourth Indiana Volunteer Infantry,* 166.

3. Lincoln was mortally wounded and Secretary of State William H. Seward badly wounded by assassins on the evening of April 14, 1865.

4. The editors have neither been able to identify nor verify this quotation.

5. Vice President Andrew Johnson, who became president upon Lincoln's death, was expected to take a hard line toward the secessionists. As it turned out, however, he treated them very leniently—too much so in the opinion of most Republicans.

6. Lee had commanded the main Confederate army in Virginia. For three years he had more or less kept the Confederacy alive.

7. Squier refers to the belief—widespread among Northerners—that Confederate authorities had plotted the murder of Lincoln. The latest research on the subject concludes that the Rebel government had hatched a harebrained scheme to kidnap Lincoln, but that the decision to kill him was made by the would-be kidnapper, John Wilkes Booth. See William A. Tidwell, James O. Hall, and David Winfred Gaddy, *Come Retribution: The Confederate Secret Service and the Assassination of Lincoln* (Jackson, 1988); and Tidwell, *April '65: Confederate Covert Action in the American Civil War* (Kent, Ohio, 1995), ch. 6.

8. Maj. Orlando J. Smith had been appointed March 23, 1864. His regiment originally had been the 71st Indiana Infantry. Smith was mustered out September 15, 1865.

9. The Confederates evacuated their capital, Richmond, Virginia, on April 2, 1865. Lee surrendered a week later.

10. Albert J. Spencer of Hall's Corners was a private in Company D. He joined the regiment February 10, 1864, and served with it until transferred to the Veteran Reserve Corps March 13, 1865. The V.R.C.—originally the Invalid Corps—was an organization composed of men who were able to perform only limited duty. It freed able-bodied men for the front-line units.

11. Lt. Lovett S. Rivenburg of the 16th United States Colored Infantry Regiment. He resigned December 4, 1865.

12. The IV Corps had been assigned to U.S. forces in the Nashville area in December. When these troops defeated the Confederates there (December 15–16), the IV Corps next pursued the Rebels as far as Huntsville, Alabama. In March 1865, the IV Corps was ordered to east Tennessee to help block any attempt by the Confederates in Virginia and North Carolina to escape to the West. In April, the Corps returned to Nashville; hence, the movement through Chattanooga.

13. On April 18, Sherman had negotiated a general surrender of all remaining Confederate forces east of the Mississippi River with Confederate Gen. Joseph E. Johnston, who surrendered on April 26. In doing so, however, Sherman had exceeded his authority and

included many matters of civil government. Sherman's agreement with Johnston aroused a storm of criticism in the North. The Federal government repudiated it and Sherman then negotiated a simple surrender of the Confederate military forces.

14. The Confederates attacked Sherman at Peachtree Creek, just north of Atlanta, Georgia, on July 20, 1864. The battle was not as close as Squier believed.

15. The Confederates attacked Sherman east of Atlanta on July 22 (the Battle of Atlanta) and suffered defeat. The Rebels, however, still held the city after that engagement and continued to do so until the night of September 1–2.

16. As indicated in the notes to Letters 6 and 7 in chapter 3, the Confederates had maneuvered north and west to operate against the railroads that supplied Sherman's army. It was Sherman, not Grant, who wanted to leave those Rebels to Thomas and march across Georgia and then up through the Carolinas. Grant finally acquiesced to Sherman's proposal.

17. At Chickamauga, about sixty-four thousand Confederates under Bragg defeated some fifty-five thousand Federals under Rosecrans. The Rebels lost about eighteen thousand men; the Yankees about sixteen thousand.

18. Rosecrans never was popular with the Northern political/military hierarchy. After his defeat at Chickamauga, he was sent to command Federal troops in Missouri. Maj. Gen. Henry W. Halleck was chief of staff of the Union armies at the time Rosecrans was sent to Missouri.

19. Pvt. John W. Gustin of Hall's Corners joined the company February 10, 1864.

20. Probably Pvt. Horace Gustin of Hall's Corners, who served in the company 1861–63 and then was discharged. See Letter 10, chapter 2.

21. Gen. Joseph E. Johnston, commanding Confederate forces in North Carolina, had surrendered to Sherman on April 26, 1865. See note 13 above.

22. This reads as if Ellen had thought herself to be pregnant but had discovered she was not.

23. Prov. 13:15.

Letter 4

[Chattanooga, May 4, 1865]

Today the remains of our late President was cons[i]gned to the narrow house, the place apointed for the whole of mankind. All busines was suspended. Flags draped in mourning [were] displayed at half mast. Nearly every doore in town wore the badge of grief. There was twenty one mi[nut]e guns fired comme[n]cing at 12 n. The guards had orders to arrest all persons who were at all noisy and boisterous. Men passing along the street laughing and jokeing were imediately "taken in out of the wet." Everything betokened the deep grief of the people. We feel the loss moore than any calamity which has befallen the nation for the last four years. The defeats at the battles of Bulls Run, the failure of the Peninsular Campaign of 1862, or the defeat at Chancello[rs]vill[e] sink into insignificance when compared with the loss which we have so recently sustained.[1] Abraham Lincoln has passed forever from our sight, but his memory will *never* pass away. Side by side with our Washington, his name will be revered so long as there is an American people. The wind is blowing so that I shal have to quit writing. I should very much like to fill this sheet. I feel like writing but the candle "flairs" so that I can scarcely see, and this must go out tomorrow morning or you may have to go two weeks without a letter, and I know you would rather have a short letter than none t'all. Tell Wilber that pa thinks of his little man very often, and Allice—the dear, noble, warmhearted girl—how I love her. And our darling little Ella, poor child, how I pitty her. I often think of the dear creature and how she has suffered. Need I tell you Darling that I think of you allways. May the day soon come when I can have you allways with me.

The news of the evacuation of Mobile is received here to day.[2] It certainly can be but a few months at farthest that we shal be kept in the field. We certainly will be mustered out by the time the drafted men in the regiment go out, which will be in October or November. But how I quit or rather how I don't quit. Good night Darling. Good night little ones.

G.W. Squier

44th Ind. Inft.

The boys are well. Saml. Hartle[3] is much better than he has been for the past ten months. Luis is "all right"—fat as a pig.[4]

G.W.S.

Will you excuse this very short epistle? Perhaps I may do better next time. That is, I may not use so much paper to write simply nothing at all.

G.W.S.

1. The reference is to four major Union defeats in Virginia in 1861, 1862, and 1863.
2. The Confederates were forced to evacuate Mobile, Alabama, on the night of April 11–12.
3. See Letters 1 and 3, chapter 3, and their accompanying endnotes.
4. Unidentified except by context.

LETTER 5

Head Quarte[r]s Co. "D" 44th Ind. Inft.   Chattanooga May 11th, 1865

My own Dear Ellen,

It is a cold a[nd] dreary night for the middle of May and in the "Sunny South" to[o]. How I wish I was seated by your side in our own dear home, with the little ones playing so merily. Am not quite homesick but am in a great hurry to get home to *stay.* Your letter mailed the 4th was received this morning. I am at loss to account for your not getting a letter two weeks ago today, as I am sure it was mailed the usual day. I generally calculate my letters to go through in Eight days, but in that instance it must have been mislaid. Of course you got it last mail, so it is now hardly worth while to mourn over it. I am going to give you the *reliable* camp news for a day or two to give you an idea of how camp life goes. To day the news is that all twelve months men are to be mustered out imediately and the three years regiments are to be reo[r]ganized and retained in the service until the expiration of their term of inlistment. Of course, this makes the vets feel rather wormey, for there is no report so absurd, but there are some who believe it. I made up my mind some time since that we would be at home by the 1st of July, possibly a little before that time but not much. The Mexican scheme is now attracting considerable attention. Thousands of men who have been in the army for three years are eager to embark in this enter-prise. For my part, I want to see the Monroe doctrine enforced, but wish to be ex-cused from takeing an active part in the affair. So you need have no fears of my embarking in that undertaking.[1] It is so cold that I shal have to go to bed to keep from freezeing. Sam[2] is grunting again with his old complaint—diarhea and sever pain in the stomach and bowels. My health is good. Good night my Love. May you sleep warmer that I expect to.

Friday, May 12th is pleasant and comfo[r]tably warm. I did not sleep. [W]as cold last night as I expected to [be] when I went to bed. Had three wool blankets over me, and of course oug[h]t not to freeze. The news to day is that the company com-manders have the muster out and discharge blanks for the regiment, so the boys are in high spirits.

Four years ago, Jefferson Davis was in the then capital of his boasted Southern Confederacy. Then he was all boasting menace and defiance towards the Northern mudsils. Then he greeted our call "to arms" with "roars of laughter." Then his "chiv-alry" would smite down every acursed yankee who dared desecrate the sacred soil of the fair South with his poluting foot. No Northern vandal should step within the limits of his confederacy and live. Four years are past—long, weary years. Four years of blood and death, of sufferings and hardships untold. And to day he is a fugitive, an outlaw with a price set upon his head, hunted down like the despised negro of former days.[3] Jefferson Davis must by this time have arrived at the conclusion that the way of the rebellion is not so easy as he proclaimed it four years ago at Mont-gomery. There is now not one from Jef down to the meanest private who is not a hunted runaway or a suppliant craving mercy at the feet of their injured country-men. Let there be no mercy for traitors and assassins. Let justice be meted out to these arch-devils full and complete. Let them suffer the extreme penalty of the law. Let criminals feel and the world know that crime will be punished. Let there be *no* mercy extended towards the worst men who ever cursed the Earth with their damnnable deeds, deeds which the most hardened criminal should turn from in horror. Out-raged justice cries for vengence. The million of widows and orphans cry for vengence. Two hundred thousand of our brethren who are maimed for life crie for vengence.

And the graves of moore than half a million of our country's defenders who have fallen in defence of liberty and law crie for vengence. And shal not vengence be visited upon their acursed heads? If not vengence, then at least give them justice one and all.

Saturday night, May 13th is delightful, just warm enough for comfort in one's Shirt sleeves. The news of the day is that the Colonel has received sealed orders for the 15th. Of cours, this means that on that day or imediately thereafter we are to be mustered out. I have lived so long in Tennessee that I take quite an interest in her public affairs, and was really rejoiced when the revised state constitution prohibiting slavery was adopted by the people, supposing it to be an end to acursed inst[it]utions.[4] But a bill establishing the "status" of the colored people of the state which has passed the lower House of the State Legislature dispels the illusion. It appears very hard for the chivelry even in the noble state of Tennessee to recognize in the negro the rights of men. I will send you the bill as it passed, even at the risk of *"boreing"* you. Taking you at your word that anything which interests me will entertain you, as I have not anything else to write about I will scribble a few comments upon that *noble document* of honorable men.[5] With [the] first section I have no objection.[6] Section second is unobjectionable except the word *free* which implies that there are other than free men in the *free* state of Tennessee when the people have decided that there shal be no slavery within its borders.[7] Section three is all right except that it excludes colored children from public schools with children of white people, and allso the word *free.*[8] Section four I find no fault with except the persistent word *free.*[9] Section five is an outrage, a downright insult to an enlightened and free people. It is returning to the old system of slavery after a so[v]ereign people have declared against it. County courts are to have the power to "bind out the children of free persons of color" without any limit whatever. Every colored child in the state may thus be "bound out." The framers of this bill neglected to state *what* color children must be to escape their parental regard. How yellow must the skin be to secure the fatherly care of thes[e] wise men who are legislating for a free people in a free state? Surely these men must forget that slavery is among the things that *were.*[10] In section six the ever present but in this cone[c]tion obnoxious word *free* occurs.[11] Section seven denies the rights of citizenship to "free persons of color" as though they were [not] as good as their late masters.[12] As regards section eight I would say that no punishment is to[o] great for the crimes spoken of. But why should there be any distinction made as to the complexion of the parties committing them? Is it so much worse for a "free person of color" to commit a crime than for one of the boasting chivalry to be guilty of the same act?[13] Section nine may be a little onesided, though not particularly objectionable.[14] Section ten seems unnecessary, for doubtless Tennessee in common with other states has a law for the punishment of vagrants. And why should the color of the vagrant make him more odious in the eyes of the law or of the community?[15] Section eleven is a direct infringement upon the rights of the "housekeepers" of the state. Is the legislature to decide who I may entertain as guests or otherwise, and how long? Surely this is freedom with a vengence.[16] Sections twelve[17] and thirteen[18] read very well, but the phrase "return to other counties and states the poor and indigent free persons of color" might exclude all emigration of "poor free colored people" to the state of Tenn. Section fourteen is unjust to the "free people of color." If there are any parties in the state who are disturbers of peace, let all of them, irrespective of color, be registered and held responsable for their acts. And then let there be no *fee* for registering these suspicious characters.[19] With section fifteen I have no objection.[20] This legislation for a certain class looks rather bad in a free state where there should be laws for the punishme[n]t of all offenders without distinction of condition or color. Let us hope that the good sense of the Senate and the firmness of Go[vernor] Brownlow[21] may defeat this abomnable bill.[22] Well I will stop here, for I know that you despise everything in shape of politics, and it is really *mean* in me to persicute you so with something which you care nothing for. It is now quite late, perhaps half past eleven, so I had better retire to my virtuous couch. Good night Nelly Dear.

A teleg[r]am received to day announces the surrender of Genl. Johnston and his army, but the report needs confirmation.[23] But where, O! Where is the once renowned Jefferson Davis? Echo answers "where." He lacked the courage to die upon the battle field. He dared not meet manfully the fate of his followers. He might have shared the fate of his army and perished with it. If he had done so, he might possibly have extorted a good word from his northern friends, and perhaps even the South might have forgiven a part of his sins. But Jefferson Davis had not the courage to surround himself with even this questionable virtue. He has shown to the world that he is a *coward* as well as a traitor and an assassin. He f[led] from Richmond and left thousands of me[n] behind to die, that he might save his own life. Like a criminal as he is, he left his strong hold and like a traitor, a coward, and a dastard, he forsook his army in their time of troubles.[24] The Eulogists of Genl. Lee will say that to stop the further effusion of blood he surrendered his army—magnanimous man, quintessence of Southern chivelry! When his army became utterly demoralized from defeat and want of necessary suplies, when he was entirely surrounded, every avenue of e[s]cape closed, when surrender or annihilation was inevitable, when death by starvation or *yankee* bullets was stareing him in the face, when any other course would have [been] suicide—to "save the further effusion of blood" he proposes to capitulate. And for this, men are lauding him to day for being a humane man, a "perfect gentleman." *I admire his courage and acknowledge his superior Generalship, but despise the man.* I look upon him as not only a traitor to his country, but a *murder[er], an assassin.* Upon analyzing my feelings towards Davis and his confederates in crime, I find something of which heretofore I have been an entir stranger—a *deep, dark hatred,* not only of their acts but the men themselves. I know that this is wrong, but knowing this does not change my feelings. Perhaps time may work a change for the better. Davis the arch traitor, the incarnate fiend, the murderer of three hundred thousand men—the man who raised the paricidal hand to strike the death blow to our free Institutions— is now doubtless on his way to Mexico, leaving his deluded people to their fate. He staked his all in a desperate game. He has lost and may now well seek oblivion in a foreign country. I'm "en emost friz" so I will turn in and perhaps by morning will get thawed out. Good night.

Sunday night, [May] 23 [21]. So cold that I am sitting with my overcoat on. Such cold weather here is entirely out of season and makes me feel like emigrating still further South. There is nothing like frost, but the wind is so chilly that one can scarcely keep comfortable without fire, even with a goodly allowance of clothing. Well, President Johnston has spoken, and though he has not definitly defined what shal be his future policy, he has said enough to convince any one that his will be milk and water policy. His speach to Ill. delegation has the ring of the true metal. He says in speaking of the murder of our late President "such a crime springs not alone from one individual of ever so despe[r]ate a character." As I wrote in my 1st Epistle general that Davis and his confederates in crime were the instigators in the foul act, Johnson says "we can trace its career back through sucessive steps to the source which is the spring of all our woes." And in the same connection he says that if the perpetrator of the fiendish act be arrested, he should suffer the extreme penalty the law knows for crime in place. He says that the American people must be taught that *treason is a crime* and will surely be punnished. He further says that shal we allow men to attempt the life of the state with impunity?[25] Such are the sentiments spoken by our Chief Executive, and to *me* they are highly satisfactory, partly because they accord with my views as previously expressed, and because I think justice now demands a stern policy. Let justice full and complete be delt out to *all* the principals in this Infamous war, which has scourged our land for the past four years and half. Let the American people know that there is law and that it *will be enforced,* cost what it may of blood and treasure. I hope that my feelings towards those incarnate fiends is not sinful, but if it is so I am sure that I know of *no* means of changeing them. Thinking over the scourges which we as a nation and as indi[viduals] have endured at their hands, I often find myself grating my teeth in real anger. Vile and infamous wretches would[. . . .]

Now here goes for the rebel army west of the Mississippi and the Mexican Emperor. According to the latest news, the Trans-Mississippi rebels are not subdued by the complete distruction of their armies in the East. It appears that they are determined to continue the war, and if reports be correct, the rebel leader is about entering into negotiations with the one horse Emperor Maximillian.[26] If that be so, it may delay the disbanding of our armies for some time. But there is nothing alarming about it, as the unequal contest proposed would inevitably result in their rapid and complete reduction and subjugation. You doubtless know my feelings on this subject, which is that it would be no cause for regret if the two should couple themselves togeather. Are they not both enemies of our government? And are they not very suitable companion[s]? And do they not deserve to have waged against them an unrelenting war? And if necessary, I would not hesitate to annihilate the whole gang of traitors and cut-throats. I can hardly believe that Maximillian is fool enough to entangle himself with the remains of the Souther[n] Confederacy. He surely ought to have moore sense than to cumber himself with that loathsome putrefying carcass. But if he should, it would be propper caus[e] for great rejoiceing among his enemies in this country. It would be the death knell of his allready precarious power on this continent. Those who desire to see him driven from his usurped throne would raise a war cry that would reverberate throughout the land and be repeated by every friend of Republicanism in all nations. Every human, whether in the new or old world, would know that his fate was sealed, that the usurper would be driven from his throne, that another great battle for human rights had been fought and won, and that oppression had received another heavy blow in our own dear America. America—may she soon become the land of the free in its broadest sense. May we live to see the oppresser, whether individual or national, be humbled in the dust.

I know that a great many good men are disbelievers in the Monroe doctrine, but should there be a war between the United States and the bogus Empire, many of these would accept it as meet and if needs be fight for it. There are others who receive this doctrine as true and would not fight for it, and your husband is one of that number.

Tuesday, May 23. Rode out in the country about four miles to day. It was truly refreshing to get out of town and once moore breathe the pure air of the country. As I am somewhat fatigued, perhaps I had better adjourne, so good night.

Wednesday. As the road from Nashville to Louisville is somewhat impaired by recent heavy rains, I do not look for your letter before Saturday, but I must not del[a]y sending this out on that account. As I am feeling very dull, it will be of no use [to] to try to write much. Your remittence came. Very good, as I had borrowed just that amt. of Henry Kessler, and of course he will need it when he leaves. His papers have not come back yet but are expected soon. Col. Curtis is now absent on leave for twenty days. The weather is getting rather warm for comfort, and everything is distressingly dull. Give love to all the friends, especially mother. If I was there, I would kiss you and the children. As it is, of course, I shal have to wait until some future time. As ever, your own husband

G.W. Squier

Has Father settled those debts with Withers?[27]

1. During the Civil War, the French government sent troops to Mexico and imposed on that country as its emperor Archduke Ferdinand Maximilian. The Federal government protested the action as a violation of the Monroe Doctrine but, preoccupied with the South's insurrection, could take no forceful steps to expel the French. After the Confederates' surrender, the Federal government sent fifty thousand troops to Texas. The French abandoned Maximilian. Mexican patriots overthrew and executed him.
2. Sam is unidentified except by context.
3. Confederate President Jefferson Davis fled Richmond when that city was evacuated on April 2. He tried to reestablish a seat of government in Virginia, then in the Carolinas, and, finally, to cross the Mississippi to reach Rebel forces still holding out. U.S. troops eventually captured him May 10, 1865, near Irwinville, Georgia.
4. A convention in Nashville in January had adopted two amendments to Tennessee's constitution abolishing slavery and forbidding the enactment of laws recognizing the right of property in men. These proposals were ratified by popular vote on February 22.
5. This refers to House Bill 47, *A Bill in Relation to Free Persons of Color*, introduced April

25 by Representative Edmund Cooper of Bedford County. The bill was referred to the Committee on Freedmen. It passed the House on May 8 by a vote of 38–18. The Senate did not pass it. See *House Journal of the First Session of the General Assembly of the State of Tennessee, 1865, Which Convened at Nashville, Monday, April 3* (Nashville, 1865), 4, 47, 80, 125–26, 130; *Senate Journal of the First Session of the General Assembly of the State of Tennessee, 1865, Which Convened at Nashville, Monday, April 3* (Nashville, 1865), 114, 117, 119; *Nashville Daily Union,* May 5, 1865.

The copy of the bill that Squier sent to Ellen no longer accompanies the letter. The Tennessee State Library and Archives holds both the original manuscript bill and a printed copy. Regarding Squier's oft-expressed objection to the word *free,* it should be noted that at the time of the debate over the bill, slavery still existed in the remaining loyal slave states and that the law may have been worded so as not to apply to any slaves who might have been brought temporarily into Tennessee from them.

6. Section 1 recognized the legality of marriages "by and between free persons of color" and prohibited marriages "by and between a white person and a negro, mulatto or person of mixed blood, to the third generation inclusive."

7. Section 2 recognized divorces between "free persons of color."

8. Section 3 granted to "married [black] women, widows, and children" coverage by the laws that applied to those groups of whites, "[p]rovided, however, that nothing in this Section shall confer upon the children of free persons of color, the rights or privileges of attending at the same public schools with the children of white persons."

9. Section 4 covered the "rights[,] duties[,] and obligations" of guardians and wards "who are free persons of color." It placed such persons on the same plane as white guardians and wards.

10. Section 5 applied only to black children. The section did enjoin the courts "to see that the apprentice is fully guarded and protected, during his apprenticeship."

11. Section 6 gave county courts the power to select a white person as the "guardian or master" for a black ward or apprentice "instead of a free person of color." Note that Squier's objection is to the adjective "free," *not* to the fact that a black child could be placed under the control of a white.

12. Section 7 provided that to be legally binding, a contract between a white and a free person of color had to be written out and witnessed by a white person. "In the event said written agreement, contract, note or memorandum is lost or mislaid, . . . the free person of color, so losing, may prove the contents of said lost instrument, by any competent white person."

13. Section 8 stipulated "[t]hat all offences made capital by the laws of this State when committed by a white person, shall be capital when committed by a free person of color." It also decreed that any free person of color who raped or attempted to rape a white female, or had or attempted to have sexual intercourse with a white female under the age of twelve, "shall suffer death by hanging."

14. Section 9 provided that for all infractions of the law other than those covered by section 8, free persons of color "shall be tried and punished in the same way, and to the same extent, as if the offenses had been committed by white persons." It also permitted blacks

to serve as witnesses "in all State Cases for or against free persons of color for crimes or misdemeanors committed against the State."

15. Section 10 provided for the punishment of black vagrants. It included a provision that specified that blacks convicted of vagrancy could be hired out to the highest bidder "for a length of time sufficient" to pay the cost of their trial. The section made no reference to white vagrants.

16. Section 11 prohibited housekeepers from "harbor[ing] such [see note 15 above] idle and worthless free persons of color" for more than five days and imposed a fine of twenty dollars for each offense.

17. Section 12 required each county to provide a "Poor House" for its "indigent poor." It specifically limited each county's responsibility to its own poor and authorized the county courts to return to their homes poor freed persons who entered the county from elsewhere.

18. Section 13 provided that the state's laws concerning "Bastards and Bastardy" would apply "in full force" to free persons of color.

19. Section 14 required "all free persons of color of age, whether male or female," to enroll in the office of the county clerk. Each registrant would receive from the clerk a "certificate printed in neat form, showing the facts." The clerk would receive a fee of twenty-five cents from each freed person who registered.

20. Section 15 required freed persons "now living as husband and wife" to procure a marriage license and have the marriage ceremony performed "so as to free them from the danger of being punished under the law for lewdness." The section authorized "any regular colored preacher, of any of the religious denominations" to perform the ceremony.

21. William G. Brownlow, an outspoken antisecessionist editor from east Tennessee, left the Confederacy during the war. He returned to the state with the invading Federal army and became governor in 1865.

22. As indicated above, the Senate did not pass the bill.

23. See Letter 3, notes 13 and 21.

24. Davis was many things, but he was not a coward. As he fled Richmond, Davis remained hopeful that he could still rally the Confederate forces and win independence.

25. President Andrew Johnson made the speech to a delegation from Illinois on April 18. The speech may be found in Leroy P. Graf, ed., *The Papers of Andrew Johnson*, vol. 7, *1864–1865* (Knoxville, 1986), 582–85. See also Letter 3, note 5.

26. See note 1 above. The Trans-Mississippi Confederates surrendered on May 26, 1865.

27. Unidentified except by context.

LETTER 6

Head Quarters Co. "D" 44th Ind. Chattanooga, July 1865

Dear Ellen,

Your good long letter mailed 6th inst. is rcd. and read with interest. In some respects I differ with you in opinion. Of course, there is nothing wrong in that. We need never expect to be of one mind in all respects, however desireable it may seem. Individuals of different education and different temperament must sometimes necessarily look at things in [a] different light and consequently arrive at different conclusions. I don't know that I shal write much on the subject of Negro sufferage, as since the policy of the President has developed I had entirely dismissed the subject from my mind.[1] A month since I might have written my reasons moore intelligibly, for at that time I thought of little else. Whatever I may say, I wish it understood that there is no offence intended in speaking of parties or principals. I shal have no reference to you. The fact is I should not attempt to discuss the subject were it not in hopes that I might show some palliating circumstances, why I am "so far behind the age in which we live." Were all the world beside of one opinion, that simple fact could make no change in my mind. This may be foolish [and] weak, but I can't help it and will throw the responsibility back on dame nature[. . . .]

[. . . .]our equals in *politics* nor can they become so except by Legislation in the states in which they reside. But what was the real mission of these unscrupulous men [and] disappointed politicians? It *was to organize a hybrid party on the platform of Negro suffrage.* And in order to ingratiate themselves with the Southern masses, the "radicals" are now and have been endeavoring to procure pardon for complicity with the rebellion. [They have] scattered[?] promiscuously and profess to be in favor of a lenient policy, hopeing thus to secure the patronage of their late erring brethren. The "radicals" were very earnest in their e[n]deavor to impress upon the mind of President Johnson the idea that a large portion of the loyal people of the United States were in favor of conferring on the negro the privilege of the elective franchise. But he failed to see it for what it was—simply an act entirely out of his jurisdiction. And for failing to overstep his constitutional powers, these gentlemen have seen fit to deno[u]nce him as pro Slavery in his policy. I am not a little surprised to see men high in office stoop to play the part of politician. Even Chief Justice Chase[2] has been flying around the country sullying the ermine of his high office in laying plans for this new party. When I see this political cunning in pursuit of power, I become disgusted with the action if not the principals which they advocate. Wendell Phillips[3] declares that if the privilege of voting is not confered upon the freedmen, he is in favor of repudiating the whole of the war debt, the solemn pledges of the government to the people, because forsooth if the negro is not allowed to vote, this war with its conseq[u]ent debt and loss of life is of no avail. In fact, it has proven an entire failure. For the past four years we have only had a series of failures. The supremacy of the law haveing been established is simply nothing. "War has only brot us a heritage of war." Poverty, shame, death, and disgrace. The nation is not benefited thereby humanity does not rejoice from the downfall of tyranny and slavery. To me this seems absurd, and yet I know as well as you do that the mass of the people North is of this opinion. The press of the south (a portion at least) as well as North advocate this doctrine. We cannot glance over the morning papers without seeing in bold letters "Relics of barbarism," "outrage upon humanity," "slavery not yet dead," or something of that sort. Beneath you will read of some Genl. Officer issueing an order prohibiting the negro from being out after a certain hour at night. Some time since I noticed an article severely censureing Genl. Halleck for issueing such an order for the government of the post of Richmond. That order was very hard on the negro indeed.[4] But in the delightful little village of Cleveland, not thirty miles from this place, a bell is rung every night before 9 P.M., and all white men or women must stay at home after that hour or they will be arrested and severely punished. And a similar order is in force at this post, and yet not one has expressed any great sympathy for the people of these places. No one appears to think the people of Cleveland or Chattanooga particularly oppressed and downtroden. I only refer to this in order to show the undue importance or rather *promine[n]ce* that is being given at the present time to every little incident that can be turned into a charge of hatred of an oppressor toward the freedmen. In fact, I am often put in mind of a favorite expression with father— "Nigger on the braine." Do not think I look at this matter lightly and as a subject of little importanc, for it would be far from the truth. I have endeavored to lay aside all prejudices and preconceived notions of "negro inferiority." I have tried to look the matter fairly and squarely in the face, comeing to conclusions from the best information which I had, which I am free to admit is decidedly limited. I know that in any case ignorance is but a poor plea for error, yet perhaps the impossability to get reading matter of the most deserved kind may be *some* excuse to *you* for my groveling position on this subject. There is one thing very sure. In this matter at least I am entirely conscien[t]ious. As it is bed time and I am somewhat fatigued I will postpone any further remarks until some more convenient season. Good night "Nellie."

1. Johnson first set forth his policy on black suffrage in his proclamations reestablishing civil government in the Southern states. By the terms of these proclamations, the right to vote for officials in the states would be limited to those who had taken the oath of amnesty and who were qualified to vote under the laws in force when the states seceded. This latter provision, of course, excluded blacks. See Graf, *The Papers of Andrew Johnson*, 136–38.

2. Salmon P. Chase, chief justice of the Supreme Court, long advocated civil rights for blacks.

3. Wendell Phillips, a longtime champion of abolition, civil rights for blacks, women's rights, and other reforms, was especially displeased by President Johnson's stand on black enfranchisement. See Irving H. Bartlett, *Wendell Phillips: Brahmin Radical* (Boston, 1961), 296–97; James Brewer Stewart, *Wendell Phillips: Liberty's Hero* (Baton Rouge, 1986), 266–71; and Oscar Sherwin, *Prophet of Liberty: The Life and Times of Wendell Phillips* (New York, 1958), 522–51.

4. Halleck at that time commanded the military division of the James. It is unclear to what incident Squier referred. On May 5 and June 12, 1865, Halleck issued general orders (No. 6 and 10) charging post commanders with preserving good order in their commands, directing them to establish an apprentice system for "minors not cared for by their parents," and referring appropriate matters to the local courts. Squier may have commented on these orders.

Selected Bibliography

∾

Army Register of the Volunteer Forces. Reprint, Gaithersburg, Md.: Olde Soldier Books, 1987.

Bailey, John C. W. *Allen County Gazetteer, Containing a Directory of Fort Wayne City, and Historical and Descriptive Sketches of the Several Townships of the County.* Chicago: John C. W. Bailey, 1867.

Bartlett, Irving H. *Wendell Phillips: Brahmin Radical.* Boston: Beacon Press, 1961.

Basler, Roy P., ed. *The Collected Works of Abraham Lincoln.* New Brunswick, N.J.: Rutgers Univ. Press, 1953.

Baxter, Nancy Niblack. *Gallant Fourteenth: The Story of an Indiana Civil War Regiment.* Indianapolis: Guild Press, 1980, 1991.

Butler, M. B. *My Story of the Civil War and the Under-ground Railroad.* Huntington, Ind.: The United Brethren Publishing Establishment, 1914.

Cooling, Benjamin Franklin. *Forts Henry and Donelson: The Key to the Confederate Heartland.* Knoxville: Univ. of Tennessee Press, 1987.

Cozzens, Peter. *No Better Place to Die: The Battle of Stones River.* Urbana: Univ. of Illinois Press, 1990.

Graf, LeRoy P., ed. *The Papers of Andrew Johnson.* Vol. 7, *1864–1865.* Knoxville: Univ. of Tennessee Press, 1986.

Griswold, B. J. *The Pictorial History of Fort Wayne, Indiana.* Chicago: Robert O. Law Company, 1917.

Helm, Thomas B. *History of Allen County, Indiana, with Illustrations and Biographical Sketches of Some of Its Prominent Men and Pioneers.* Chicago: Kingmen Brothers, 1880.

Holt, Michael F. *The Political Crisis of the 1850s.* New York: John Wiley and Sons, 1978.

House Journal of the First Session of the General Assembly of the State of Tennessee, 1865, Which Convened at Nashville, Monday, April 3. Nashville: S. C. Mercer, 1865.

Josyph, Peter, ed. *The Wounded River: The Civil War Letters of John Vance Lauderdale, M.D.* East Lansing: Michigan State Univ. Press, 1993.

A Library of Poetical Literature in Thirty-Two Volumes. Vol. 1. New York: American Home Library, 1902.

Long, David E. *The Jewel of Liberty: Abraham Lincoln's Re-election and the End of Slavery.* Mechanicsburg, Pa.: Stackpole Books, 1994.

McDonough, James Lee. *War in Kentucky: From Shiloh to Perryville.* Knoxville: Univ. of Tennessee Press, 1994.

Official Roster of the Soldiers of the State of Ohio in the War of the Rebellion, 1861–1865. Akron, Ohio: Werner Ptg. and Mfg. Co., 1888.

Remini, Robert V. *Andrew Jackson and the Course of American Empire, 1767–1821*. New York: Harper & Row, 1977.

Report of the Adjutant General of the State of Indiana. Indianapolis: W. R. Holloway, 1865–66.

Rerick, John H. *The Forty-fourth Indiana Volunteer Infantry: History of Its Services in the War of the Rebellion and a Personal Record of Its Members*. Lagrange, Ind.: John H. Rerick, 1880.

Scott, Walter. *The Lady of the Lake: A Poem*. 2d ed. Edinburgh: John Ballantyne and Co., 1810.

Senate Journal of the First Session of the General Assembly of the State of Tennessee, 1865, Which Convened at Nashville, Monday, April 3. Nashville: S. C. Mercer, 1865.

Sherwin, Oscar. *Prophet of Liberty: The Life and Times of Wendell Phillips*. New York: Bookman Associates, 1958.

Smith, John David. "Yankee Ironclads at Birkenhead? A Note on Gideon Welles, John Laird and Gustavus V. Fox." *The Mariner's Mirror* 67 (February 1981): 77–82.

Stampp, Kenneth M. *Indiana Politics During the Civil War*. Indianapolis: Indiana Historical Bureau, 1949; reprint, Bloomington: Indiana Univ. Press, 1978.

Stewart, James Brewer. *Wendell Phillips: Liberty's Hero*. Baton Rouge: Louisiana State Univ. Press, 1986.

Stillwell, Yvette M. "The Forty-Fourth Indiana Volunteer Regiment: Federal Forces, 1861–1865." Unpublished seminar paper, North Carolina State Univ., June 1995.

Supplement to the Official Records of the Union and Confederate Armies. Wilmington, N.C.: Broadfoot, 1994.

Sword, Wiley. *Shiloh: Bloody April*. Dayton, Ohio: Morningside, 1983.

Terrell, W. H. H. *Indiana in the War of the Rebellion: Report of the Adjutant General*. Indianapolis: Indiana Historical Society, 1960.

Thornbrough, Emma Lou. *Indiana in the Civil War Era, 1850–1880*. Indianapolis: Indiana Historical Bureau & Indiana Historical Society, 1965.

———. *The Negro in Indiana Before 1900: A Study of a Minority*. Bloomington: Indiana Univ. Press, 1993. Originally published 1957.

Tidwell, William A. *April '65: Confederate Covert Action in the American Civil War*. Kent, Ohio: Kent State Univ. Press, 1995.

Tidwell, William A., James O. Hall, and David Winfred Gaddy. *Come Retribution: The Confederate Secret Service and the Assassination of Lincoln*. Kent, Ohio: Kent State Univ. Press, 1988.

The United Methodist Hymnal: The Book of United Methodist Worship. Nashville: The United Methodist Publishing House, 1989.

Valley of the Upper Maumee River, with Historical Account of Allen County and the City of Fort Wayne, Indiana. The Story of Its Progress from Savagery to Civilization. Vol. 1. Madison, Wis.: Brent & Fuller, 1889.

The War of the Rebellion: A Compilation of the Official Records of the Union and Confederate Armies. Washington: Government Printing Office, 1880–1902.

Willey, Robert. *The Iron 44th*. N.p., n.d.

Index

෪

This Wilderness of War was designed and typeset on a Macintosh computer system using PageMaker software. The text and titles are set in Adobe Garamond. This book was designed by Todd Duren, composed by Angela Stanton, and manufactured by Thomson-Shore, Inc. The recycled paper used in this book is designed for an effective life of at least three hundred years.